My mother said I must always be intolerant of ignorance but understanding of illiteracy. That some people, unable to go to school, were more educated and more intelligent than college professors.

Maya Angelou

Life is the most exciting opportunity we have. But we have one shot. You graduate from college once, and that's it. You're going out of that nest. And you have to find that courage that's deep, deep, deep in there. Every step of the way.

Andrew Shue

My best friend is the most important girl, outside of family, to me. I met her when I went to college and we bonded immediately. I'd do anything for her at any time. We phone each other every day.

Dawn French

A college degree is the key to realizing the American dream, well worth the financial sacrifice because it is supposed to open the door to a world of opportunity.

Dan Rather

You know what has made me the happiest I've ever been? Seeing my son and daughter graduate from college. More than wanting them to be educated, I wanted them to be nice people. To see that they have become both is just a wonderful thing.

Gil Scott-Heron

At a time when going to college has never been more important, it's never been more expensive, and our nation's families haven't been in this kind of financial duress since the great depression. And so what we have is just sort of a miraculous opportunity simply by stopping the subsidy to banks when we already have the risk of loans. We can plow those savings into our students. And we can make college dramatically more affordable, tens of billions of dollars over the next decade.

Arne Duncan

I spent three days a week for 10 years educating myself in the public library, and it's better than college. People should educate themselves - you can get a complete education for no money. At the end of 10 years, I had read every book in the library and I'd written a thousand stories.

Ray Bradbury

You don't have to be a genius or a visionary or even a college graduate to be successful. You just need a framework and a dream.

Michael Dell

A thorough knowledge of the Bible is worth more than a college education.

Theodore Roosevelt

Education is the key to the future: You've heard it a million times, and it's not wrong. Educated people have higher wages and lower unemployment rates, and better-educated countries grow faster and innovate more than other countries. But going to college is not enough. You also have to study the right subjects.

Alex Tabarrok

My dad was in the army. World War II. He got his college education from the army. After World War II he became an insurance salesman. Really, I didn't know my dad very well. He and my mother split up after the war. I was raised by my maternal grandmother and grandfather, and by my mother.

Al Pacino

When we make college more affordable, we make the American dream more achievable.

William J. Clinton

It is virtually impossible to compete in today's global economy without a college degree.

Bobby Scott

The American Dream is one of success, home ownership, college education for one's children, and have a secure job to provide these and other goals.

Leonard Boswell

Mentors provide professional networks, outlets for frustration, college and career counseling, general life advice, and most importantly, an extra voice telling a student they are smart enough and capable enough to cross the stage at graduation and land their first paycheck from a career pathway job.

Gerald Chertavian

You are graduating from college. That means that this is the first day of the last day of your life. No, that's wrong. This is the last day of the first day of school. Nope, that's worse. This is a day.

Andy Samberg

By the way, intelligence to me isn't just being book-smart or having a college degree; it's trusting your gut instincts, being intuitive, thinking outside the box, and sometimes just realizing that things need to change and being smart enough to change it.

Tabatha Coffey

If you want to get laid, go to college. If you want an education, go to the library.

Frank Zappa

By making college unaffordable and student loans unbearable, we risk deterring our best and brightest from pursuing higher education and securing a good-paying job.

Mark Pocan

When I was in college, I wanted to be involved in things that would change the world.

Elon Musk

It's something you dream about as a kid. Like when you play all those NCAA video games as a kid and you create your own player and win the Heisman with a bunch of crazy numbers. It's the biggest, most prestigious award in college football, so it'd definitely be a dream come true.

Johnny Manziel

Ignoring fame was my rebellion, in a funny way. I was insistent on being normal and doing normal things. It probably wasn't advisable to go to college in America and room with a complete stranger. And it probably wasn't wise to share a bathroom with eight other people in a coed dorm. Looking back, that was crazy.

Emma Watson

No one should be denied the opportunity to get an education and increase their earning potential based solely on their inability to pay for a college education.

Bobby Scott

The Black Panther Party was not a gang. They grew out of a young black intelligentsia on college campuses.

Bobby Seale

Growing up, I was a little hippie kid. I went to some good concerts... Amnesty International with Bob Dylan and Tracy Chapman... The best concert I ever went to was this one at the Cow Palace my freshman year in college on New Year's Eve. It was Pearl Jam opening for Nirvana opening for Red Hot Chili Peppers.

Summer Sanders

I've had tendinitis since college.

Michael Jordan

College is a refuge from hasty judgment.

Robert Frost

I would counsel people to go to college, because it's one of the best times in your life in terms of who you meet and develop a broad set of intellectual skills.

Bill Gates

I don't believe we are supposed to go through life defeated and not having enough money to pay our bills or send our kids to college.

Joel Osteen

I believe that God's dream is that we be successful in our careers, and that we be able to send our kids to college. I don't mean that everyone is going to be rich, and I preach a lot on blooming where you're planted. But I don't have the mindset that money is a bad thing.

Joel Osteen

If we choose to keep those tax breaks for millionaires and billionaires, if we choose to keep a tax break for corporate jet owners, if we choose to keep tax breaks for oil and gas companies that are making hundreds of billions of dollars, then that means we've got to cut some kids off from getting a college scholarship.

Barack Obama

I don't have a college degree, and my father didn't have a college degree, so when my son, Zachary, graduated from college, I said, 'My boy's got learnin'!'

Robin Williams

I made my first white women friends in college; they loved me and were loyal to our friendship, but I understood, as they did, that they were white women and that whiteness mattered.

Alice Walker

I met Howard Zinn in 1961, my first year at Spelman College in Atlanta. He was the tall, rangy, good-looking professor that many of the girls at Spelman swooned over.

Alice Walker

I started writing as a child. But I didn't think of myself actually writing until I was in college. And I had gone to Africa as a sophomore or something - no, maybe junior - and wrote a book of poems. And that was my beginning. I published that book.

Alice Walker

My mother had bought a sewing machine for me. When I went away to college, she gave me a sewing machine, a typewriter and a suitcase, and my mother made $17 a week working as a maid 12 hours a day, and she did that for me.

Alice Walker

October is a fine and dangerous season in America. a wonderful time to begin anything at all. You go to college, and every course in the catalogue looks wonderful.

Thomas Merton

A lot of parents today are terrified that something they say to their children might make them 'feel bad.' But, hey, if they've done something wrong, they should feel bad. Kids with a sense of responsibility, not entitlement, who know when to experience gratitude and humility, will be better at navigating the social shoals of college.

Amy Chua

I learned more about the economy from one South Dakota dust storm that I did in all my years of college.

Hubert H. Humphrey

After my first year of college, each course I took in every field was so boring that I didn't even go to the classes.

Noam Chomsky

Anyone can be a moral individual, concerned with human rights and problems; but only a college professor, a trained expert, can solve technical problems by 'sophisticated' methods. Ergo, it is only problems of the latter sort that are important or real.

Noam Chomsky

All my way through college, I worked my way as a window dresser for Lord & Taylor, so I always liked fashion. I always loved fashion and I love that we can do it and not take it seriously.

Joan Rivers

You can't learn to write in college. It's a very bad place for writers because the teachers always think they know more than you do - and they don't. They have prejudices. They may like Henry James, but what if you don't want to write like Henry James? They may like John Irving, for instance, who's the bore of all time.

Ray Bradbury

I don't think there's been anything in the game of football in my lifetime that has changed college football more than redshirting.

Lou Holtz

People like bluegrass. It's had a following amongst a lot of hip and young people. A lot of college kids like bluegrass.

Dolly Parton

If you look at the history of Notre Dame, if you hire a coach who's been successful at another college program, they're going to be ultra successful at Notre Dame because the talent will always be there.

Lou Holtz

I've met graduating college kids facing loan payments and a bad economy, and they are worried that they won't be able to get a job. This is not the way America needs to be.

Mitt Romney

One of the great mind destroyers of college education is the belief that if it's very complex, it's very profound.

Dennis Prager

When I was in college, I really liked poetry. I don't read much anymore.

Steve Martin

See, that's why Barack's running: to end the war in Iraq responsibly - to build an economy that lifts every family, to make sure health care is available for every American - and to make sure that every child in this nation has a world-class education all the way from preschool to college.

Michelle Obama

When I was in college, I was debating to try my hand at show business, or to become a professor. I just thought of the risk of not going into show business and always wondering if I would've had a chance. Because that's where my real heart was.

Steve Martin

Walking has been ridiculous in college basketball the past 15 years.

Bobby Knight

What I tell my kids is, 'I'm preparing you for college and for life. So, having independence, knowing how to set your own boundaries, figuring out how to make that balance. We still have screen-time rules.'

Michelle Obama

A white boy that makes C's in college can make it to the White House.

Chris Rock

Generally young men are regarded as radicals. This is a popular misconception. The most conservative persons I ever met are college undergraduates. The radicals are the men past middle life.

Woodrow Wilson

I always wanted to be some kind of writer or newspaper reporter. But after college... I did other things.

Jackie Kennedy

I didn't do improv in college, I never performed, I didn't do theater either. I was in student government, I was a history major.

Demetri Martin

As compared with the college politician, the real article seems like an amateur.

Woodrow Wilson

In high school, a teacher once suggested that I be a math major in college. I thought, 'Me? You've got to be joking!' I mean, in junior high, I used to come home and cry because I was so afraid of my math homework. Seriously, I was terrified of math.

Danica McKellar

If you think the President was right to open the doors of American opportunity to young immigrants brought here as children who want to go to college or serve in the military, you should vote for Barack Obama.

William J. Clinton

After I left high school and got my GED, I studied broadcast journalism for a year at a community college.

Chris Rock

The idea of going back to college scares me, and I didn't even go. I went to college for one year, two semesters. If you add up the total time, I probably didn't even go one semester.

Rush Limbaugh

Malcolm X found the language that communicated across the board, from college professor to floor sweeper, all at the same time, without demeaning the intellect of either.

John Henrik Clarke

When I was in high school and college, I thought everybody could think in pictures. And my first inkling to my thinking was even different was when I was in college and I read an article about, you know, some scientist said that the caveman could not have designed tools until they had language.

Temple Grandin

The new American dream is one of responsibility. What is the bottom-line number that you're going to be able to pay back toward a student loan responsibly if you're doing it yourself after you have a job? That dictates the amount of money you can borrow. That dictates the school you can go to, if you can even go to a four-year college at all.

Suze Orman

People like me who grew up in a working-class town, who don't have a college education, you don't usually hear from us.

Michael Moore

Ooh, it's too embarrassing to share my innermost romantic secrets - although I have written Danielle the odd poem. If anything they are more comedic than romantic. They used to be well-received but that was before she started studying Shakespeare at drama college. Now I feel so inept.

Gary Lineker

Language for me narrates the pictures in my mind. When I work on designing livestock equipment I can test run that equipment in my head like 3-D virtual reality. In fact, when I was in college I used to think that everybody was able to do that.

Temple Grandin

I thought I would, you know, go to college, get to law school, finish, and then get a job and work as a lawyer, but that proved to be not a good fit for me.

Demetri Martin

There's great disparity between who goes to college and who goes to jail. Who lives long and who dies prematurely, is the defining issue of our time. And I submit to you, there's a significant race dimension, it is basically class-driven.

Jesse Jackson

I took my kids everywhere. I didn't have money for child care, so I took them to college with me and they sat in the hallway.

Iyanla Vanzant

The funny guy doesn't get the girl until later in life. High school, college, everyone still wants the brooding, dangerous guy you shouldn't have.

Will Ferrell

Mostly I want to talk positive; I wanna talk about a bunch of great kids that I coached and made me look good and the university that I've seen grow from a cow college, which it was, only 12,000 people, and when I came here, we weren't at Pennsylvania State University, we were at Penn State College.

Joe Paterno

I went to college because I didn't have anywhere else to go and it was a fabulous hang. And while I was there I was exposed to this world that I didn't know was possible.

Tom Hanks

It is not hard for me to remember when I was in college. I loved many things about college life: I loved learning. I loved the comradery. And I loved football.

Joseph B. Wirthlin

My mother raised me in the church. I was not allowed to stay home on Sunday; there was no option. I sang in the choir all the way up until I went to college.

Steve Harvey

I was an English major in college, and then I went to graduate school in English at the University of North Carolina for three years.

Elizabeth Edwards

I did my first apprenticeship when I was 15, then joined the union when I was 17. I worked every summer in high school and college.

Christopher Reeve

My grandfather worked in a shoe factory - he was an Italian immigrant. My father was the first to go to college in the family.

Camille Paglia

College is a place to keep warm between high school and an early marriage.

George Gobel

I like college football, but I'm a huge college basketball fan. I could sit and watch every game of March Madness and be happy. That could be a vacation.

Lewis Black

Academics, who work for long periods in a self-directed fashion, may be especially prone to putting things off: surveys suggest that the vast majority of college students procrastinate, and articles in the literature of procrastination often allude to the author's own problems with finishing the piece.

James Surowiecki

And then it was like, wait, you can go to college and study theater? And act in plays? This is almost a racket, you know. And then when the opportunity came along to do it professionally, I thought I'd won the lottery.

Tom Hanks

I was supposed to be too short to play college volleyball.

Summer Altice

I had a lot of friends in high school and in college, and we had a good time.

Ricky Williams

It was well after college that I learned about depression. I got my first job for Jack Paar. I realized I was sleeping 14 hours a day and just living for the Paar show.

Dick Cavett

When I was in college I did a lot of stupid things and I don't want to make an excuse for that. Some of the things that people accuse me of are true, some of them aren't. There are pranks, IMs.

Mark Zuckerberg

Universities used to prepare young adults for the real world. I dare say the graduates today go in without a clue and graduate without a clue. It's time to acknowledge the college degree is not worth what it was in the past. Times are changing, and so is the way we prepare our youth to survive in a competitive world.

Dale Archer

I stand before you as the governor of Texas but also stand before you the son of two tenant farmers. Ray Perry who came home after 35 bombing missions over Europe to work his little corner of land out there and Amelia who made sure that my sister Milla and I had everything that we needed, included hand sewing my clothes until I went off to college.

Rick Perry

I get letters from college kids who have read Percy Jackson when they were younger who tell me, 'I just passed my Classics exam.' The books are accurate enough that they can serve as a gateway to Homer and Virgil.

Rick Riordan

No matter what, your parents are going to worry about you. I had a tour bus, and my mother still thought I was broke. Remember: It's your life, not theirs. Just because your parents sent you to college doesn't mean they bought the rest of your life.

Lewis Black

One of the big concerns I have is that most of the HR departments in a lot of companies are hiring away from creativity and they don't know it. For instance, they are requiring everybody to have a college degree. The most creative people I know couldn't deal with college.

Nolan Bushnell

I guess when people ask what is the biggest transition to the NBA from college, it is definitely defense and the mental part.

Magic Johnson

Being 5' 10, I was supposed to be too short to play college volleyball. So that gave me the hunger and the fire to say, Oh yeah? I'd just hit the crap out of the ball.

Summer Altice

All students should have the opportunity to receive their high school diplomas and be fully prepared for college or the workplace.

Magic Johnson

My most lucrative job in college was a stint as the regional Dodge Girl.

Jessica Savitch

I would gladly have accepted a heaping spoonful of nepotism when I got out of college and was looking for a job.

Sloane Crosley

As a small child in England, I had this dream of going to Africa. We didn't have any money and I was a girl, so everyone except my mother laughed at it. When I left school, there was no money for me to go to university, so I went to secretarial college and got a job.

Jane Goodall

If you want to surf, move to Hawaii. If you like to shop, move to New York. If you like acting and Hollywood, move to California. But if you like college football, move to Texas.

Ricky Williams

My dad had been shortstop when he was in college, and you know, when you're a kid, you want to be just like your dad.

Derek Jeter

During the 1980s, when Japan's economy was roaring and people were writing books with titles like 'Japan is Number One,' most Japanese college students didn't make the effort to become fluent in English.

Rebecca MacKinnon

I had tried to go to college, and I didn't really fit in. I went to a real narrow-minded school where people gave me a lot of trouble, and I was hounded off the campus - I just looked different and acted different, so I left school.

Bruce Springsteen

I dropped out of high school and I couldn't go to college 'cause I wasn't smart enough, so I'd resigned myself to loading trucks and playing punk rock on the weekends.

Dave Grohl

If I had spent as much time in the weight room as I did designing football uniforms, I probably would have had a free college education.

John Malkovich

When I was in college, I had a jazz radio show. I called it 'Excursion on a Wobbly Rail,' after a Cecil Taylor song. I used to run around the Village following Ornette Coleman wherever he played.

Lou Reed

One goes through school, college, medical school and one's internship learning little or nothing about goodness but a good deal about success.

Ashley Montagu

I went to Northwestern because I had gone to a really nontraditional high school. I was like, 'It'd be cool to have a traditional college experience.' Then I was like, 'Oh, but none of these people understand what's cool about me. My specialness is not appreciated in this place.'

Zooey Deschanel

My dad was an immigrant kid and a Democrat and a Jew, and we didn't know any Republicans in our group. So I grew up Democratic. My dad was a labor lawyer - a very hardworking guy, a one-horse labor lawyer - and then I went to hippie college and lived in the bubble.

David Mamet

I love to box. I once took a kickboxing class in college and got totally hooked.

Sophia Bush

Americans are the only people in the world known to me whose status anxiety prompts them to advertise their college and university affiliations in the rear window of their automobiles.

Paul Fussell

I wasn't the high-school play queen or anything. And my parents would let not me act until I graduated from college.

Gwyneth Paltrow

I took part in a theater festival in Massachusetts two summers after I graduated from college. Then I was in Los Angeles, thinking, 'I am going to go to New York.' So I bought a plane ticket and found a place to live and packed my bags. And suddenly, a week before I was supposed to leave, I had three job offers - and one of them was my first movie.

Chris Pine

As far as I was concerned, the Depression was an ill wind that blew some good. If it hadn't occurred, my parents would have given me my college education. As it was, I had to scrabble for it.

Sargent Shriver

By the time I was ready for college, I didn't know what I wanted to do. I think I secretly wanted a show business career, but I was suppressing it.

Will Ferrell

I had the most incredible English and literature teachers in school, and it really influenced my love of storytelling. It's what made me excited to study journalism in college. I love editorials and documentaries. All of that came from being given the opportunity to lose myself in good writing when I was a kid.

Sophia Bush

My mother taught public school, went to Harvard and then got her master's there and taught fifth and sixth grade in a public school. My dad had a more working-class lifestyle. He didn't go to college. He was an auto mechanic and a bartender and a janitor at Harvard.

Ben Affleck

My early childhood prepared me to be a social psychologist. I grew up in a South Bronx ghetto in a very poor family. From Sicilian origin, I was the first person in my family to complete high school, let alone go to college.

Philip Zimbardo

Last I looked - and I'm not a candidate - but last time I checked reading about the Constitution, the Electoral College has nothing to do with parties, has absolutely nothing to do with parties. It's most states are winners take all.

Michael Bloomberg

The experiencing self lives in the moment; it is the one that answers the question, 'Does it hurt?' or 'What were you thinking about just now?' The remembering self is the one that answers questions about the overall evaluation of episodes or periods of one's life, such as a stay in the hospital or the years since one left college.

Daniel Kahneman

I regret to this day that I never went to college. I feel I should have been a doctor.

Ty Cobb

There is nothing better than to make it to the College World Series. All of the extra reps in the weight room, all of the early morning practices, and all the hard work spent the entire year makes it worth it.

Jennie Finch

For students today, only 10 percent of children from working-class families graduate from college by the age of 24 as compared to 58 percent of upper-middle-class and wealthy families.

Patrick J. Kennedy

In college, I think I probably positioned myself as an aspiring writer, meaning I dressed sort of extravagantly and adopted all the semi-Byronic affectations, as if I were writing, although I wasn't actually doing any writing.

Anthony Bourdain

I don't believe in writer's block. Think about it - when you were blocked in college and had to write a paper, didn't it always manage to fix itself the night before the paper was due? Writer's block is having too much time on your hands.

Jodi Picoult

This is a value-added college education if I have heard one described. And what is the most remarkable about Delaware State University graduates - is they just keeping giving back.

Michael N. Castle

When people ask where I studied to be an ambassador, I say my neighborhood and my school. I've tried to tell my kids that you don't wait until you're in high school or college to start dealing with problems of people being different. The younger you start, the better.

Andrew Young

They're on the right road, but there's a long way to go on concussions, not only in the NFL, but college football, high school football and all football.

John Madden

I dropped chemistry. I practically blew up the lab in college.

Patricia Cornwell

After college, I knew I wanted to work in comedy, so the first thing I did was go to where the comedy was. I moved from Charlottesville to Chicago, because that's where The Second City and Improv Olympics are. You have to go wherever you need to go to study what interests you.

Tina Fey

Yeah, I did some small parts in high school and the first year of college and then fairly soon thereafter I settled into the backstage scenery, and then at the University of Maryland I was doing posters for their productions.

Jim Henson

In the '50s and '60s, journalism wasn't a profession. It wasn't something you went to college for - it was really more of a trade. You had a lot of guys who came up working in newspapers at the copy desk, or delivery boys, and then they would somehow become reporters afterward and learn on the job.

Matt Taibbi

I think going to college for that one year was probable the best thing I have ever done.

Carmelo Anthony

I joined an improv group in college, which was a lot of fun. After I graduated, I moved to Chicago to try to get into the Second City.

Steve Carell

I majored in screenwriting and playwriting in school - and wanted to make films as a career. But when I directed my first short in college - which was called 'Extras' - I lost thousands of dollars and made an unsatisfying and incomplete film.

Mike Birbiglia

I went to school and made good grades and went to college. So I was afforded an opportunity through my parents' hard work that most people don't have.

Anthony Mackie

It's funny, I get a little quieter with time. I don't want to chase my tail and one day repeat myself and repeat myself and one day have kids going to college and not have memories that I should, because I was too busy doing my thing.

Dave Matthews

I grew up in Chicago, so I've always been a Bears fan. Dad used to take me to Bears games and Cubs games. My brother used to ride me over to Lake Forest College on his Honda Supersport and we'd watch the Bears practice. I remember those guys out there as monsters - they were the biggest things I've ever seen!

Kyle Chandler

I wasn't using college as a stepping stone to law school or some other career. I just wanted a liberal-arts education.

Charlie Trotter

Sometimes you're a little too close for comfort, and I think anybody can relate to that, whether you're in college or just moving out on your own.

Leighton Meester

Some of the best projects to ever come out of Atari or Chuck E. Cheese's were from high school dropouts, college dropouts. One guy had been in jail.

Nolan Bushnell

Though I didn't quite plan it that way, I had my two sons at just about the same ages my mother saw me and my sister off to college, and my first novel was published when I was 46. This 'tardiness' isn't something I'm proud of, but I'm happy to be an inspiration to others who arrive at these milestones later than most of us do.

Julia Glass

Right around the end of the fifties, college students and young people in general, began to realize that this music was almost like a history of our country - this music contained the real history of the people of this country.

Jackson Browne

Our great history has been that people came to Michigan because you didn't have to have a college degree to get a good-paying job. Consequently, we have got a larger number of our population that right now are facing outsourcing, et cetera, without higher or advanced degrees.

Jennifer Granholm

President Obama once said he wants everybody in America to go to college. What a snob.

Rick Santorum

I was always a good student, but I didn't read that much until I was 18 and I was working my way through college.

James Patterson

The morning after my high-school graduation found me up early job hunting. The dream of college I put on the back burner.

Martha Reeves

Our record number of teenagers must become our record number of high school and college graduates and our record number of teachers, scientists, doctors, lawyers, and skilled professionals.

Ruben Hinojosa

One half who graduate from college never read another book.

G. M. Trevelyan

My father was a trained accountant, a BCom from Sydenham College and a self-taught violinist. In the 1920s, when he was in his teens, he heard a great violinist, Jascha Heifetz, and he was so inspired listening to him that he bought himself a violin, and with a little help from an Italian teacher, he learned to play it.

Zubin Mehta

Usually, girls weren't encouraged to go to college and major in math and science. My high school calculus teacher, Ms. Paz Jensen, made math appealing and motivated me to continue studying it in college.

Ellen Ochoa

The senior thesis of Hillary D. Rodham, Wellesley College class of 1969, has been speculated about, spun, analyzed, debated, criticized and defended. But rarely has it been read, because for the eight years of Bill Clinton's presidency it was locked away.

Bill Dedman

When God saved me, He gave me a thirst to learn and to read and to study. I thrived in college. I got a bachelor's degree in philosophy and then went to Reformed Theological Seminary in Orlando.

Tullian Tchividjian

Although professors regard improving critical thinking as the most important goal of college, tests reveal that seniors who began their studies with average critical thinking skills have progressed only from the 50th percentile of entering freshmen to about the 69th percentile.

Derek Bok

When I got to college, acting suddenly seemed like a very risky proposition and all my friends were going to law school or med school or Wall Street.

Wentworth Miller

My first few films were institutional comedies, and you're on pretty safe ground when you're dealing with an institution that vast numbers of people have experienced: college, summer camp, the military, the country club.

Harold Ramis

I love football. My weekends are booked. Saturday college games and Sunday NFL and 'Monday Night Football.' Booked! Football is first, then basketball and then everything else.

Jordin Sparks

One very clear memory I have of college is that I never learned anything in the big lectures. I have a feeling I'd have done even worse if they'd been on a laptop screen.

Gail Collins

When I came home for the summer after my first year of college, I told my mother that my best friend and I were driving to California. She laughed out loud - 2,000 miles in a what? Well, my best friend had an old Chevy. What could go wrong?

Jane Smiley

I speak as much Spanish as anyone who has grown up in Southern California or Texas or Arizona. I had my three years of high-school Spanish and a couple of semesters in college.

Will Ferrell

I played guitar and bass. I didn't do much vocals, although I did have one band where I was the lead singer. But that was when I was in college.

Oscar Isaac

I was fighting every windmill, especially when I was in college.

Bill Parcells

We also knew it would be difficult, because of the financial condition of the family, for me to go to college.

Alan Shepard

On the rare occasions when I spend a night in Oxford, the keeping of the hours by the clock towers in New College, and Merton, and the great booming of Tom tolling 101 times at 9 pm at Christ Church are inextricably interwoven with memories and regrets and lost joys. The sound almost sends me mad, so intense are the feelings it evokes.

A. N. Wilson

You know, bad poetry I wrote in high school can still be found on the Internet, and, you know, there's a Web log of our college newspaper. You know, there's so many different stages of my creative development are sort of on-record if somebody were to choose to look for them.

Lena Dunham

I have lovely memories of Los Angeles in the 1930s. I came down to live with my mother's cousin and they invited me to come and go to junior college for a year.

Beverly Cleary

Do you realize that if we could increase just by 50 percent the number of adults who have a college degree, it would add $5 billion to the economy and it would result in a net income to the state of Arkansas of $340 million a year?

Mike Huckabee

My very first gig was with the Sex Pistols, and it was also our first-ever gig. It was a very short set, and it was at Saint

Martins College of Art in 1975. We were opening up for a band called Bazooka Joe, and their bass player at the time was Adam Ant, who went on to form Adam and the Ants.

Steve Jones

My youngest uncle Randy and I were the first members of our entire family to ever go to college.

James Earl Jones

More than ever, a college diploma unlocks economic opportunity, provides students with a wealth of new skills and knowledge, and encourages innovation and growth. But more than ever, it also comes with a mountain of student loan debt.

Mark Pocan

When I was in college my girl got me a job at the doctor's office she was working at. I was a file clerk. No disrespect but I don't think a man can do that job. It takes so much meticulous and precise file-keeping.

J. Cole

The college graduate is presented with a sheepskin to cover his intellectual nakedness.

Robert M. Hutchins

I hang out with a lot of the people I did when I was in high school, when I was in college, and I have a strong unit of people around me, whether it be friends or family, and if my head gets too big, they will definitely check me immediately.

John Cena

It's difficult to not be able to just be yourself without criticism in any position, whether you're in high school, college, or this industry.

Raven-Symone

I don't know if I'd ever want to show my college life in the films I make. I think I've passed that stage long ago.

Anurag Kashyap

In my brief sojourn in college, my favorite classes were political science because I loved the idea of systems we can set up that benefit society - rules we can put in place that sometimes you run against, sometimes they're painful, but ultimately they benefit the world.

Matt Mullenweg

When I enrolled in college at age 19, I had a total of eight years of formal classroom education. As a result, I was not comfortable with formal lectures and receiving regular homework assignments.

Philip Emeagwali

After I graduated from college, while traveling around Europe, hitchhiking, doing the tourist thing, I went into a church in Dublin.

Frederica Mathewes-Green

I went to the University of San Francisco on an athletic scholarship. I didn't study in high school. I was just there to get by and to play basketball. But a funny thing happened to me when I got to college. I got challenged by the work and the professors.

Michael Franti

I can't read music. Instead, I'd do stuff inside the piano, do harmonics and all kinds of crazy things. They used to put me in these annual piano contests down at Long Beach City College, and two years in a row, I won first prize - out of like 5,000 kids! The judges were like, 'Very interesting interpretation!' I thought I was playing it right.

Eddie Van Halen

I'm constantly trying to make myself better, to learn more. I didn't finish college, so I feel like I'm always having to prove myself. I don't want to feel like the smallest person in the room.

Nina Dobrev

I don't attend an actual school but I'm still following through with high school. I do work with a tutor for about six hours a day. It's hard core but definitely worth it, and it's my main focus now - finishing up high school before I release my new album and apply to college.

JoJo

In my family, there was one cardinal priority - education. College was not an option; it was mandatory. So even though we didn't have a lot of money, we made it work. I signed up for financial aid, Pell Grants, work study, anything I could.

Eva Longoria

It's kind of like a college degree... when you get one, no one can take it from you. When you get to say for the rest of your life that you've got a platinum album, that really means something.

Luke Bryan

Especially girls, but any kids exposed to music programs and arts programs do much better on their tests. They have a better chance of going to college. They can focus better. You know, we're not just automatons learning how to work machines and do engineering and math and science. All of that's great, but you've got to build a whole person.

Bonnie Raitt

I don't want players coming in from the college level that are either trying to avoid a suspension, declare themselves ineligible on their own, hire an agent and decide, 'I'm going to enter into the NFL.'

Roger Goodell

I paid my way through college as a carpenter and a woodworker. So I've built the house I live in and most of the furniture that's in it, and I do a lot of woodworking still.

Misha Collins

The lopsided attitudes of college professors pose a serious challenge to learning because students are so susceptible to becoming lopsided sheep.

Suzanne Fields

When I give speeches at college, I don't tell stories, I talk about what it is to live your dreams and take the path less traveled.

Tucker Max

I like art with a sense of humor. I don't have a huge art education to understand everything. I don't think that means that art has to be watered down to the lowest common denominator, though. I don't think you have to go to college to be able appreciate great art, but I like art that doesn't take itself too seriously.

Kathleen Hanna

Coming out of college into the draft, being Asian-American and being from Harvard, that's not going to be an advantage because of stereotypes.

Jeremy Lin

I see a young man playing 'Plaisir d'Amour' on guitar. I knew I didn't want to go to college; I was already playing a ukulele, and after I saw that, I was hooked. All I wanted to do was play guitar and sing.

Joan Baez

I don't think most people understand that when I wasn't running for president, I was working. Because I have to earn income. I have three kids in college. And three in school. And I have a little girl that has a lot of special needs. So I've got to work for a living. I was working already.

Rick Santorum

You know, I have a lot of books on my iPad, but when I try to read them, I find myself wandering off to play games. Those are books I'm interested in. I can't imagine what would have happened to me in college if my biology class had been on the same computer as 'Words With Friends' and 'Doom.'

Gail Collins

This sounds like a brag, but I know how to make good fried rice. I learned in college. There are two secrets - take the rice after you cook it and let it get cold in the fridge. Then cook the egg like you're making a fried egg and just before it's done, dump the rice and veg on it and swirl it around.

Patton Oswalt

I'm a lesbian. Yup. Hundred percent. Hundred percent. I remember being in college, and I had fallen in love with this woman, and I remember sitting in my dorm room saying out loud to myself, like, 'You have enough problems. You are not gonna let this happen.' You just kinda, like, stuff it away until - well, some people stuff it away forever.

Christine Quinn

When I tell people I work to stop hazing in high schools I am almost always met with shocked expressions. 'High school? Really? I thought that was something that only arrogant frat guys do in college.' But it's true - as long as I have worked on preventing bullying in high schools, I have worked to prevent hazing.

Rosalind Wiseman

I just think winners win. And guys who won all the way through high school and college, the best player at every level, they have a way of making things happen and winning games.

Tony Dungy

Everybody in my family had a real sick, twisted sense of humor. Most of the jokes we make in our house, we would just never even dream of making anywhere else. Just sick, horrible stuff. That wasn't anything new to college.

Seth MacFarlane

When I was in school, my mother stressed education. I am so glad she did. I graduated from Yale College and Yale University with my master's and I didn't do it by missing school.

Angela Bassett

I particularly enjoy cello music because our daughter plays the cello. I have listened to her practice for so many hours that I am familiar with the music written for that instrument. I am also fond of the popular music of the 1930s because my future husband and I danced to it so many Saturday nights when we were in college.

Beverly Cleary

I enjoyed the whole process of learning and was always happy when autumn came and school or college started up again.

Claire Tomalin

Everyone has a different path. I knew no one in the acting industry growing up. I never did a play until college. I was not outspoken when I was younger and I hated being the center of attention. But I had a dream of being an actor. I went to NYU and studied theatre. I learned a craft. And began my career straight out of college.

Peter Facinelli

A telephone survey says that 51 percent of college students drink until they pass out at least once a month. The other 49 percent didn't answer the phone.

Craig Kilborn

At our college we were taught a universal approach to find out about a person: what problems the person has, what difficulties, what personal tendencies and likings.

Markus Wolf

Maybe everyone is a little too reassuring that things are going to be OK to college graduates. It gives them a false sort of security.

Peter Dinklage

After I dropped out of college at the age of 19, I became a mortgage broker, and when I went back to school I thought about going into real estate law. I probably would have made a lot more money and died of boredom by now.

Alice Dreger

I wasn't going to be a college kid. The only subject I was interested in was English. I think I had a subconscious interest in analyzing story.

Eric Bana

For some reason the football coach of a major college program is seen as one of the leaders of the campus. And some way we have to let our young people know that that leader can look like anyone.

Tony Dungy

It is not my wish to lounge about the college and fatten on a fellowship all my days. I am always trying to look upon a college life as a medium not an end.

Thomas Edward Brown

I tried college for three months but I was desperately unhappy. I just wanted to perform. I was getting straight As but I had no friends and cried every day.

Keira Knightley

It was like a heart transplant. We tried to implant college in him but his head rejected it.

Barry Switzer

It occurred to me in my junior year of high school. I got my first letter from a big college. I still have that letter to this day - a letter from Indiana.

Bo Jackson

I didn't get to college until my 20s, because I was a young father on welfare and had to take all kind of jobs to support my young son. There's what frames my view on the topics I discuss on my shows, and the average person relates to that. No matter how many degrees I have now, I lived that life, and that comes through to the people watching.

Michael Eric Dyson

My son was born during my last semester in college. His due date was Thanksgiving, but he didn't show up until finals week. I brought my books to the hospital and didn't think anything of it. That is what a father is supposed to do.

LZ Granderson

My grandmother is a huge Hawkeyes fan, so I, by proxy, have to be one. I'm more of a professional sports fan, and I've never been a huge college fan, but because of my grandmother, I've gotten into a lot of really good Hawkeye games. So, because I'm a good grandson, I'm a Hawkeye fan.

Corey Taylor

I went to college because I felt like I was supposed to. I graduated from public high school and I did all the things that I was supposed to do.

Mila Kunis

I didn't know any successful actors in Kenya, so I felt like I could get away with going to college to study film more easily than I could with saying, 'I want to be an actor.' That's what I did.

Lupita Nyong'o

I've been programming computers since elementary school, where they taught us, and I stuck with computer science through high school and college.

Masi Oka

An employer would be a complete fool to let an image like college partying influence their hiring decisions.

Nick Denton

By the time I was at college, I became very alert to the question of racial discrimination, and I remember one of my first writing attempts had to do with a lynching.

Albert Maltz

I abandoned chemistry to concentrate on mathematics and physics. In 1942, I travelled to Cambridge to take the scholarship examination at Trinity College, received an award and entered the university in October 1943.

John Pople

After college, rather than pursue real work, I joined a folk group and sang in coffee houses and nightclubs, an occupation that does little for the intellect and even less for the complexion.

Marshall Brickman

I've participated in many demonstrations since I was a child. When I was at medical college, I was fighting King Farouk, then British colonization, against Nasser, against Sadat who pushed me into prison, Mubarak who pushed me into exile. I never stopped.

Nawal El Saadawi

Most of my friends from college became dental hygienists or went into retail, a lot went into sales. They all started getting married and having kids and buying homes and I was still living like a college student.

Patricia Heaton

I remember coming to this college in the 1960s as a new legislator when a road divided the campus - and it was not fully paved at that - and no wall defined the campus from the highway.

Michael N. Castle

I was the first boy in the Kennedy family to graduate from college.

Mark Kennedy

I went to my dad when I was 17 and said, 'I want to be a country music star.' Which every dad loves to hear. And he said, 'I want you to go to college.' So we had a discussion. And I'm pretty stubborn. I'm a lot like him. And he said, 'If you go to college and graduate, I'll pay your first six months of rent in Nashville.' So he bribed me.

Eric Church

I always knew I wanted to be an entrepreneur. I started my own software company in high school and went to college to study entrepreneurship.

Marc Benioff

You know, I never really paid attention to sports, which, coming from the mecca of football in Texas, is kind of odd. I played sports, but I was nerdy. Having a single mother, the pressure was on me to get good grades and a scholarship and go to college.

Sarah Shahi

Landing on 'Morning Joe' wasn't a fluke. I was a poli sci major in college. I interned at the CBS political unit, covered conventions.

Willie Geist

I think day care is terrific. Kids get to be around other kids, and they're playing, and they're teaching each other. When I was in college, my summer job was being a preschool teacher. I loved it, and after that experience, I said I can't wait to put my kid in day care because I could see how much they loved it.

Jessica Valenti

I had no choice but to work hard. I was a straight-A student, went to college, and I loved business. I never thought I was going to be a singer myself.

Jenni Rivera

My mother was a great typist. She said she loved to type because it gave her time to think. She was a secretary for an insurance company. She was a poor girl; she'd grown up in an orphanage, and she went to a business college - and then worked to put her brothers through school.

Robert Wilson

I used to do a lot of serious theatre during my school and college days. Comedy was only reserved for youth festival and inter-college competitions. Then once 'The Great Indian Laughter Challenge' was launched, a regional channel in Punjab started a program based on that. I participated in it and emerged as the winner.

Kapil Sharma

At one point, I was hell-bent on being a Disney animator, and sort of got over that in college and wanted to do my own stuff. You know, towards the end of college I had actually planned to go to the Boston Conservatory of Music for musical theater.

Seth MacFarlane

I dropped out of school for a semester, transferred to another college, switched to an art major, graduated, got married, and for a while worked as a graphic designer.

James Green Somerville

I always wanted to play a mental patient. I was fascinated with playing crazy people in college, and I don't know if I ever quite perfected it.

Alison Brie

Even the pictures I was doing at college - a little narrative based on a butterfly catcher, or a chimney sweep - the images were always telling stories. They were all scenarios and moods which I storyboarded and worked through - it's exactly what I do now.

Tim Walker

When I graduated from college, I went straight to work for a federal contractor, a desk job, and they were great to me, they loved me, I was like their mascot, but I just couldn't stand working in an office. I just hated it. And so one day I went in and said, 'I'm sorry, this is my two-weeks notice, I'm quitting to become an artist.'

Maggie Stiefvater

Actually, music gave me the support when I needed it. I would never have gone to college unless I'd gotten a piano scholarship. And now I'm so glad I got to learn to play the cello, which is a different experience, you're flexing a different muscle, but it's beautiful because it is music.

Jamie Foxx

We hear the stories every day now: the father who puts on a suit every morning and leaves the house so his daughter doesn't know he lost his job, the recent college grad facing up to the painful reality that the only door that's open to her after four years of study and a pile of debt is her parents'. These are the faces of the Obama economy.

Mitch McConnell

I was always most interested in drawing - most of my childhood drawings are black-and-white line work. And when I kind of abandoned comics, through college and art school, I was doing a lot of painting. But once I started doing comics again, everything else just fell by the wayside.

Jeffrey Brown

These ivy league students are in the upper echelon of the college boards and had great opportunity in front of them regardless of where they go to college. Its in their very nature and it is something they expect.

Michael N. Castle

My brother was a huge Charles Barkley fan - my brother went to Miami. He played power forward, and he always used to tell me stories about Barkley and college. And I watched Barkley growing up. I loved what he brought to the game. His toughness and just his attitude, being as strong he was.

Paul Pierce

All my friends from my past would know me as Scott Diggs. Taye Diggs comes from Scott-taye. When I went to college I liked it because it was so different and I have an infatuation with nicknames.

Taye Diggs

I got a gymnastics scholarship to college, fell in love with my true love of my whole life - who I'm married to now - and he was a virgin too. It was very romantic.

Victoria Jackson

After Watergate, which happened when I was in college, I became increasingly inspired by journalism as a way to change the world. It sounds corny, but to wake the public up, to serve a higher cause.

David Talbot

Noises and smells, those can bring back powerful memories. I remember when I was going to school one Fourth of July, and there were a lot of fireworks going off. I knew that I was in Richmond. I knew that I was a college student. But I thought people were shooting at me.

Kevin Powers

I started radio in 1950 on the Lone Ranger radio program, a dramatic show that emanated from Detroit when I was 18 years old and just beginning college. I did that for a couple of years.

Casey Kasem

I think, especially when you're in college, each book that you're reading tends to tell you who you are.

Jeffrey Eugenides

If I were put into a college lecture hall right now and told to pay attention for 45 minutes, it would be physically impossible for me to do. I'm one of those people who believe that ADD is a gift. It's tough to manage, but if you can harness it you can do great things.

Jeff Kinney

There will always be another group of kids going to college, drinking beer, and discovering that movie. Many of them have never even heard of SCTV.

Rick Moranis

Aaron and I will be joined at the hip until the day we die. We have loved and hated each other since the day he was born. He's very much a part of my heart. He's going to broadcasting college now, and he'll do fine. But he came into a world that did not welcome him.

Lynn Johnston

College was especially sweet because of the positive, hopeful atmosphere of a college campus.

Jerry Kramer

When you're a little kid, you just like music that makes you happy and is fun. As you get older, you reach college or your 20s and you decide that music should be challenging and all art should be smart. So you start to think it makes you like high art more to put down things you consider low art. I don't even think things are low art.

Patrick Stump

Even when I was young, playing college football, and I injured my knee, I bounced right back.

Lee Majors

By the time I left college, I had won every award you could win - I was Mr. Man! Then I got drafted by the Giants, and you step in that locker room, and you feel inferior in every way. You just have to stick around long enough to give yourself the opportunity to build your confidence.

Michael Strahan

Our promise to our children should be this: if you do well in school, we will pay for you to obtain a college degree.

Ruth Ann Minner

I went to the University of Arizona. I stopped because I went there for two years and I felt like I experienced college or whatever. I'm over it. I like Hollywood better.

Nicole Richie

I lived in the States from 1996 till 2000. I attended the Berklee College of Music in Boston in 1997. But I wasn't the most hard-working student. I rarely went to school. At that time, I seriously doubted that you could learn creativity in school. Music isn't something you can just learn from other people. Sometimes I regret missing classes.

Psy

For a while after college, I was thinking of becoming a fitness trainer, and I am a certified aqua trainer.

Dylan Lauren

Our obsessive focus on college schooling has blinded us to basic truths. College is a place, not a magic formula. It matters what subjects students study, and subsidies should focus on the subjects that matter the most - not to the students, but to everyone else.

Alex Tabarrok

My parents had an old-fashioned ideal of college, that four years at a liberal arts college should be a liberal arts education.

Julie Bowen

I joined Khalsa College just opposite Don Bosco in class XI, but soon I quit studies and was sent to Bangkok by my father to learn martial arts, as that is the only place we could afford given that I would also work there to support my training.

Akshay Kumar

Gone are the days when your indiscretions at university were recorded in a roneoed college newsletter of which there is only one copy left tucked in a filing cabinet at the back of a library. Today that same college newsletter is online, accessible by the whole world now and forever.

Malcolm Turnbull

As a child, I had no idea that I would end up in the film industry. My ambitions changed from wanting to join the army like my grandfather to taking up merchant navy as a career to running for India, and finally, investment banking while I was a student of economics honour. But during my college days, I began to get offers for modelling.

Arjun Rampal

Fresh out of college, you tend to join a company because it's a job. But, you tend to stay because it becomes a career; you start to feel at home. In the beginning of your career, you're focused on you: 'I like this place because I'm doing rewarding work; they take good care of me; the people are nice; there's runway for me,' etc.

Ursula Burns

I watch HGTV like a maniac, and when it's bad, it's like some crazy college guy watching a football game.

Melissa McCarthy

I guess after college, I just got really into food. I also think going on the road doing stand-up makes you more into food. Because when you travel like that, one of the things to do is find really good places to eat.

Aziz Ansari

What college is all about is some kind of 4-year game about who is going to end up with the highest grades. And I don't mean to say that academic achievement isn't important. But it is, after all, a means to an end.

Derek Bok

I now have two kids of my own in college, so I know how important it is that we keep the dream alive for every family and I share the concern about rising tuition costs.

Mark Kennedy

My message to students is that if you want to become an entrepreneur and save the world, definitely don't skip college. But go to a school that you can afford. You'll be freed from the chains of debt and succeed on your own ambition and merit.

Vivek Wadhwa

I went to performing arts high school, and I took dance and acting every day. Then, I went to Marymount Manhattan College and I have a B.A. in acting, with a concentration in theater performance and a minor in musical theater. I studied there for three years.

Jenna Ushkowitz

When it came time to go to college, I had been accepted for Harvard when my father was offered the position of head of the Metropolitan Life Insurance Company office on the west coast, and we moved to San Francisco.

Douglass North

I used to do puppet theatre and also mime and musical theatre in Florida for competitions and festivals, which was great. I was very much involved in theatre when I was in college.

Wesley Snipes

The need for a college education is even more important now than it was before, but I think that the increased costs are a very severe obstacle to access. It is an American dream, and I think that one of our challenges is to find a way to make that available.

Roy Romer

Commencement speeches were invented largely in the belief that outgoing college students should never be released into the world until they have been properly sedated.

Garry Trudeau

I did most of my volunteer work when I was in college because I knew of more ways to get involved. In high school, we'd do things like, there was a homeless shelter near our hometown and our church group decorated one of the rooms. In college, I was in a sorority, and we did a lot of things, like pick up trash on the highway.

Carrie Underwood

I think everyone should go to college and get a degree and then spend six months as a bartender and six months as a cabdriver. Then they would really be educated.

Al McGuire

Chemistry is a class you take in high school or college, where you figure out two plus two is 10, or something.

Dennis Rodman

The aim of a college education is to teach you to know a good man when you see one.

William James

I was a terrible student. Still, I managed to get into college, but my daydreaming threatened to sabotage me. I used behavior modification to break the cycle. I started by setting an arbitrary time limit on studying: for every 15 minutes of study, I'd allow myself an hour of daydreaming. I set the alarm.

Sandra Cisneros

In my situation, every time I write a sentence, I'm thinking not only of the people I ended up in college with but my siblings, my family, my school friends, the people from my neighborhood. I've come to realize that this is an advantage, really: it keeps you on your toes.

Zadie Smith

When should a college athlete turn pro? Not until he has earned all he can in college as an amateur.

Will Rogers

I'm a good son, a good father, a good husband - I've been married to the same woman for 30 years. I'm a good friend. I finished college, I have my education, I donate money anonymously. So when people criticize the kind of characters that I play on screen, I go, 'You know, that's part of history.'

Samuel L. Jackson

Cauliflower is nothing but cabbage with a college education.

Mark Twain

It wasn't until I went to college and I got my first motorcycle that I understood the thrill of speed.

Vin Diesel

Steve Jobs, Bill Gates and Mark Zuckerberg didn't finish college. Too much emphasis is placed on formal education - I told my children not to worry about their grades but to enjoy learning.

Nassim Nicholas Taleb

Economists who have studied the relationship between education and economic growth confirm what common sense suggests: The number of college degrees is not nearly as important as how well students develop cognitive skills, such as critical thinking and problem-solving ability.

Derek Bok

Our youth deserve the opportunity to complete their high school and college education, free of early parenthood. Their future children deserve the opportunity to grow up in financially and emotionally stable homes. Our communities benefit from healthy, productive, well-prepared young people.

Jane Fonda

There were high school coaches such as Charles Boston that took me under his wing and taught me the fundamentals of football. And when I went to college there was Robert Hill who took me there and he showed me what hard work and determination would do if you put forth the effort and you take a little time.

Walter Payton

College isn't in everyone's hearts. I am living proof, though, that school doesn't mess up your plans. It gives you more experiences to write about.

J. Cole

In college, you had to worry about that math class or this exam that's coming up on Tuesday, but not in the professionals. You eat, sleep, and do everything related to your craft - and your craft is football. You can be at it from sunup to sundown.

Cam Newton

I was not a good student. I did not spend much time at college; I was too busy enjoying myself.

Stephen Hawking

In college I never realized the opportunities available to a pro athlete. I've been given the chance to meet all kinds of people, to travel and expand my financial capabilities, to get ideas and learn about life, to create a world apart from basketball.

Michael Jordan

I think a college education is important no matter what you do in life.

Phil Mickelson

I think I'm mostly looking forward to the college life. I'm looking forward to more freedom. Here everything is really structured and scheduled, but in college you've got to be more responsible and you can get things done on your own time. I'm really looking forward to that.

Nerlens Noel

I never went to college. But the structure I grew up with was planted so deep that when it came to doing business, I knew how to be disciplined, create teamwork, and persevere. It set me up to be an entrepreneur and a successful franchiser.

Anne F. Beiler

I struggled with being a broke college graduate, and while all my friends were getting career jobs, I was working horrible part-time jobs. That's why now, even when I get tired, I think, 'This is what I asked for.'

J. Cole

I never grew up thinking the goal in life was to be a millionaire. All the way through college, I had a part-time job. I worked hard to get the things that you need at that age.

Cecelia Ahern

My friends started having children after college, while I was pursuing this crazy acting career and living hand to mouth. Plus, all my boyfriends were artists struggling to make a living. Having kids didn't make any sense - why would I take on more of a financial burden when I couldn't even afford a dog?

Edie Falco

My mother is a fighter. After she battled polio and learned to walk again, the doctors told her she would be a cripple her entire life. Instead of accepting defeat, she refused this fate and went on to become the West African Women's Singles tennis champion in college.

Uzo Aduba

I went to college at Harvard, then did three years of graduate school at Yale. At both places I studied comparative literature. People find it odd that I went to both Harvard and Yale, and I guess it is odd, but that's just what people did where I grew up.

Lev Grossman

For me, the desire exists less to get myself a degree than to just go and have the whole college experience, and throw myself into the brain pool and see if I can swim.

Joshua Jackson

I would anticipate that the Electoral College will be held on the 13th of December, and our 20 electorate votes will go to the certified winner.

Kenneth Blackwell

Well, when I was younger, in high school, I started out smoking pot. Which escalated into taking acid on a regular basis, which escalated into selling acid. And then I started, when I went to college, I started doing opiates.

John Wozniak

I am not a very social person and have a few friends who have been with me since school and college. I hate going to parties and events and would rather sit at home and watch TV. Parties are the place where controversies happen.

Sonakshi Sinha

I used to go down every year for the remembrance of Elvis' birthday. Memphis State College invited me to sit in the auditorium and speak to the people for one of those Elvis days.

Otis Blackwell

School was a waste of time for me. I was bored and left at 16. I started taking correspondence courses at college instead. I did incredibly well. I won an award for my grades.

Amber Heard

Then in college, besides economics, I also majored in studio art and got involved in photography and making short films and acting. But I didn't know you could make a living that way.

Brit Marling

I hated school. After 15, you went off to college if you were good enough. It didn't appeal to me so I left school. I did what everybody did - get a job.

Tony Iommi

I think the most surprising thing about the Olympics would be the amount of interaction and partying that goes on behind the scenes. They have nightclubs at the Olympic Village. It's like college all over again.

Misty May-Treanor

I grew up in Pennsylvania in a small town. Real small, like one high school and one movie theater. Well, there was a state college there, that was the only good thing about it.

Keith Haring

Having a college degree gave me the opportunity to be... well-rounded. Also, the people I met at the university, most of them are still my colleagues now. People I've known for years are all in the industry together.

Jon Secada

I realized that the only way to get into a good college was to be valedictorian or salutatorian. So that was my goal.

Melinda Gates

A professional player is smarter than a college man. He uses his noodle. He knows what to do and when to do it. He rarely goes up in the air as is the case with most of our college players when they get in a tight place.

Red Grange

Education helps you to be a well-rounded person, period. It teaches you how to take in information and data, process it, and use it for life building. Education was key in my family. You were going to college.

Yolanda Adams

I found college useful for a lot of other reasons. It exposed me to a great many influences I wouldn't otherwise have encountered, and gave me a lot of time with some very intelligent people whose thoughts are still with me.

Walter Jon Williams

I think women as well as men are concerned about jobs and the economy and spending and, and other issues. They're concerned that when their kids graduate from college they have an economy and they have a future in this country and they, they have the same opportunity that we've had and our grandparents have had.

Ken Buck

We created a show and a scenario for college students where they can take what they learn in class every day and apply it to the real world.

Ross Martin

When I started in the press there were really ink-stained wretches. Not everybody went to college. Now, everybody at the New York Times and the Washington Post and Salon and Slate, most of them have Ivy League educations.

Joe Klein

I play trumpet. And I took all the music courses in college, so I can also play the string instruments, keyboard, the brass and woodwinds - but only well enough to teach them.

If you put a violin in front of me, you wouldn't say, 'My God, that guy can play.' It'd probably sound more like Jack Benny.

Jon Tester

I think that I always thought that if my uncle was on Broadway, then I must inherently have a good voice. I don't think that for a while I did. Eventually, out of sheer will of never wanting to get a job or go to college, I found my way into doing music full-time.

Nate Ruess

My mom didn't believe in putting chemicals in hair. But when I got to college, we didn't have A/C in our dorms freshman year. So after several days of waking up looking like a Chia Pet, I was like 'OK, I'm gonna get a perm.' And then my hair revolted and fell out. I was over that quick, fast and in a hurry.

Keshia Knight Pulliam

I love college life.

Lil' Romeo

I'm taking a philosophy class and regretting it with everything in me. I'm taking one college class per semester. Philosophy is studying what you already know and dismantling it. I thought it would be right up my alley. I can't tell you how much it's not me.

Helen Hunt

In college, I probably lost a total of about 11 games, and then I came to the Celtics and in my first three weeks we went on a nine-game losing streak.

Paul Pierce

The energy of college football rivals that of a live performance for me. I am an extremely analytical guy and predicting these games is right up my alley, especially with a little luck thrown in. It is even more fun when I am winning and I have to say, I have fared quite well in my predictions.

Rodney Atkins

At AT&T, I learned an awful lot about people, and how important it is to have the right people in the right jobs.

And when I say 'right people,' I'm not talking about their college degree or work history; I'm talking about things like bearing - How does this person interact with other people? Can he or she talk to you and not tick you off?

Edward Whitacre, Jr.

During my school and college days, the three Khans - Aamir, Salman and Shah Rukh - were superstars for me and will always be. Their movies were eagerly awaited every Friday.

Shahid Kapoor

Both of my parents graduated from high school, both attended college, both have government jobs now. They've always been very adamant about me finishing high school and finishing college.

Chance The Rapper

I chose to do comedy instead of going to college.

Bo Burnham

In high school, I worked eight hours a day just so I could get into the college of my dreams and say that I got in - and I never went.

Bo Burnham

I never thought about writing. I was married young, I was still in college, as we did then, and I had two babies before I was 25, and I loved them, and I loved taking care of them, but I was a little bit cuckoo, staying at home and not having a creative outlet.

Judy Blume

For a long time, I dressed like an idiot. In college, I had a fully shaved head with just two horns. Like, a coxcomb of hair that I would sculpt into two horns. I looked like a crazy person.

Kurt Braunohler

In college, I faced an interesting problem. I wanted to play music all the time and yet I wasn't ready for anyone to hear it. To remedy this, I took to retreating to stairwells as a safe place to sing and write music. It was there that I wrote most of my songs in college and really grew into an artist.

Kina Grannis

I had a teacher in college who drastically changed the course of my life by telling me that he believed in me as an actor. I never received that support before, and it inspired to me to such a degree that I never looked back. He taught me that it's okay to be crappy; it's okay to fight; it's okay to go to any length.

Taylor Schilling

The idea of trust-fund guys who live in Brooklyn in their 30s is really interesting to me. There's a time and a place where that kind of bohemian lifestyle is appropriate, soon after college, in your 20s. But there are people still living that many years later; they haven't evolved to the next phase.

Tim Heidecker

I learned mime back when I was in college, at Ball State University, Indiana. That woke up my body from the neck down and made me realize that acting and communication - portraying a story, event, or emotion - is a full-body experience.

Doug Jones

Your humble critic confesses that he has been wrestling with 'weight issues' since leaving college lo these, uh, several years ago, so it's hard to be receptive to the moralistic scolding and patronizing encouragement offered endlessly by the allegedly well-meaning.

Tom Shales

I was the first in my family to go to college, and I waitressed all the way through, using my earnings to pay for a bachelor's degree first and then a master's. I resented classmates who didn't have to work real jobs, the ones who had the luxury of taking unpaid internships that would eventually position them for high-paying careers.

Ali Liebegott

My love of horses began in College Park, with me and 10 friends on two couches and a keg of beer in the back of a truck, heading to Pimlico at 6 A.M. to mark our place in the middle of the Preakness infield, where we never saw a horse run.

Kevin Plank

This year, we must address the Colorado Paradox. We have more college degrees per capita than any state. Yet we lag the nation in the percentage of students who go on to higher education.

Bill Owens

I was always into fashion because my mom has always been interested in fashion. She majored in fashion merchandising in college, and it's always been something we have in common.

Dakota Fanning

I didn't finish college, which is really weird because they awarded me the Alumni of Distinction recently.

Joely Fisher

Going to Omaha for the College World Series - the people there are tremendous - huge crowds and a lot of excitement. I still remember those days - you make a lot of friends that you never forget when you win a championship like that.

Roger Clemens

I love to work with the younger kids who are trying to live out their dreams, if in fact that's what they plan on doing after college to take the next step. A very select few have that opportunity so when you do have the opportunity you know, those guys take advantage of it.

Roger Clemens

I'm afraid I talk a lot, too much, perhaps. I should have been a lawyer or a college professor or a windy politician, though I'm glad I am not any of these.

Tom Glazer

I am involved with 'Write Girl,' which is such a great organization, because they go into inner city schools and work with underprivileged girls to pair them up with other writers. And it gets them learning to express themselves and become familiar with their own voice. They have a 100% success ratio getting those girls into college.

Melissa Rosenberg

You can be 24 and continue to live like you're at college, or even continue to live like you're in high school. Or you can put on a shirt and tie and pretend to be an adult.

Ezra Koenig

My first job out of college was as an editorial assistant in a New York publishing house. Being an editorial assistant is the purgatory would-be editors must endure before they can ascend the ladder and begin acquiring books on their own. I spent a year filing paperwork, writing copy, and typing rejection letters.

Lincoln Child

No period of my life has been one of such unmixed happiness as the four years which have been spent within college walls.

Horatio Alger

When I started out in the duck-call business, my college buddies would come in and say, 'Robertson, you have a college degree. What are you doing?' Then they drove away saying, 'What an idiot!' Thirty-five years later, they're saying, 'The sucker's a genius!'

Si Robertson

So when I told my parents I wanted to go into acting because I was flunking out of my first year of junior college, they were relieved that I had picked something other than joining the army. But I can't imagine how they had high hopes for me.

Dustin Hoffman

I mean, if somebody said to me, junior year of college, you can go anywhere, your old man's paying for it, I'd have been gone in a flash. But I had to work. Every summer my mother would say, 'Get that job and hold on to it until August 30.'

Chris Matthews

I majored in geology in college but have majored in Herbert Hoover ever since.

Lou Henry Hoover

No one except Hollywood stars and very rich Texans wore Indian jewelry. And there was a plethora of dozens if not hundreds of athletic teams that in essence were insulting us, from grade schools to college. That's all changed.

Russell Means

In college, I was always disappointed by lectures that covered social problems but failed to identify what I could do to change them. Part of the problem was that many professors simply didn't believe they had a role in converting awareness to action.

Ben Rattray

In high school, a teacher's friend in the police department asked me to go into a bar and flash a fake ID saying I was 21 even though I wasn't. They were assuming the bar wasn't carding people. Anyway, she forgot to ask for it back. I used it all freshman year in college.

Betsy Brandt

I'm the first one out on the dance floor. In college I had to take jazz, ballet and tap dancing, but, before that, it was just social.

Miles Teller

And this year, when we end the cruel, defeatist practice of passing children who cannot read into fourth grade, and when our most diligent students begin to graduate from high school in 11 years, and get a head start on college costs with the dollars they earned through their hard work, others will take notice of Indiana yet again.

Mitch McConnell

I studied fashion at the London College of Fashion. I get involved in it as part of my own styling, so if I wasn't a pop star maybe a fashion buyer or a stylist.

Rachel Stevens

My father was career military. He was a veteran, he was a doctor of political science, he taught at West Point and Air Command Staff and lectured at the War College.

Suzanne Collins

College football is the only game in the country, of any kind, that the college game is longer than the pro game.

Nick Saban

When I was younger it was - you know, my dad dressed up in drag on 'Bosom Buddies.' And that was what I was having to deal with at the time. And then around the time that I was into college was when he became statue-worthy I guess you could say.

Colin Hanks

I got scars on my face that tell some kind of story. I'm looking in the mirror, and I got one scar that's really two scars - half from a baseball bat and half from playing football in college. I'll tell you, though, after a while, your face gets so wrinkled up you can hardly see them.

Kris Kristofferson

We didn't even think about it, you know? I used to collect laser discs, and you'd have some college professor analyzing It's a Wonderful Life or Citizen Kane, and now it is pretty funny - the idea of commentary for a silly kid's movie, you know?

Dana Carvey

I went to an historically black college where we're always told that there's limitation. And so I'm happy to represent for black colleges.

Terrence J

Our approach to education has remained largely unchanged since the Renaissance: From middle school through college, most teaching is done by an instructor lecturing to a room full of students, only some of them paying attention.

Daphne Koller

The normal storyline of a horror film or a slasher film is the young, beautiful college folks go camping and get systematically killed by the person in a mask. So that's how it normally is.

John Schneider

I grew up dancing, and for a while in college, I was a gym rat. I finally realized... I'm going to create a little more balance in my life and make exercise something that I enjoy doing. So I went back to dance when I started doing more musical theatre, and I've just found that it's the best thing that works for my body.

Christine Lakin

It was always my dream, to do a leading role on Broadway. It's what I went to college to do, in hopes of one day someone taking a chance on me and saying, 'You know what? You're going to be our girl.'

Patina Miller

I hadn't played any music since freshman year of college, more than thirty years ago, so I had to relearn everything. I started writing songs. Some were dance and trance songs (I listen to them a lot while I'm writing), and some were love songs, because that after all is what music is about - dancing and trancing and love and love's setbacks.

Nicholson Baker

If you have urgent current expenses to cover, then future priorities like college and retirement fall off your radar because they are simply less pressing. Scarcity of attention prevents us from seeing what's really important. The psychology of scarcity engrosses us in only our present needs.

Sendhil Mullainathan

At college I'd seen my dead frog's limbs twitch under some applied stimulus or other - seen, but hadn't believed. Didn't dream of thinking beyond or around what I saw.

James Merrill

I was a baseball player and a football player at Stanford, so I didn't play a lot of golf in college. I really started playing a lot after I turned pro and I had some time in the off-season.

John Elway

I got into the Shanghai Drama Institute because my parents, like all parents, want their children to have good grades and to go to a good college. I became a college student because of them.

Li Bingbing

But in my college years it got to the point where my friends and I didn't do anything without consuming a massive amount of alcohol before we went anywhere or did anything, and you know that.

Jim Coleman

I went to a college in New York called New Paltz. I studied theater there for four years. I also studied privately in NYC with a teacher named Robert X. Modica.

Aida Turturro

I got that experience through dating dozens of men for six years after college, getting an entry level magazine job at 21, working in the fiction department at Good Housekeeping and then working as a fashion editor there as well as writing many articles for the magazine.

Judith Krantz

I had a liberal arts education at Amherst College where I had two majors, mathematics and philosophy.

Stephen Cole Kleene

Believe it or not, the first spark for everything I've done today came down to me meeting one person in college who changed my life. A student named Anthony Adams who lived across the hall from me in our freshman dorm showed me what it meant to be an 'entrepreneur' when I saw him launch his own start-up company.

Elliott Bisnow

You have, unfortunately, a K-12 educational system where the requirements to graduate are not the requirements to be college and career-ready. So if you want young adults who are college and career-ready, our K-12 system right now does not have that as its standard.

Gerald Chertavian

Heartbreak comes in different sizes, and the departure of an 18-year-old child for a far college has to be treated as a very benign form of the disease.

Jonathan Raban

There happened to be guitar classes at the college, and there was a guitar teacher there with whom I used to play. In addition, I also would go out into country schools and teach little kids basic guitar and singing a few times a week.

Mark Knopfler

I think college prepared me at a really high level. High school, you can take some plays off on the defensive end. Not on purpose, but if your man gets tired, you can rest a little bit. But once you get to college, and especially in the NBA, you can't do that. Even if my man gives the ball up, I'm on help side, helping my team out.

Trey Burke

My dad grew up in a working-class Jewish neighbourhood, and I got a scholarship from my dad's union to go to college. I went there to get an education, not as an extension of privilege.

Ezra Koenig

I feel like 'Gossip Girl' isn't really 'Gossip Girl' anymore when they're away at school because they don't go to NYU; they go to, like, Yale and Brown. New York City is just as much a character as anyone else in the books, and I was really sort of reluctant to show them off in their separate college worlds.

Cecily von Ziegesar

I feel so gratified about having finished college. I learned how to articulate myself. It gave me confidence more than anything. And also the ability to analyze the text.

Maggie Gyllenhaal

When I was in college there was a girls' flag football league. The girls were extremely aggressive.

Lynn Swann

The obsessive focus on a college degree has served neither taxpayers nor students well. Only 35 percent of students starting a four-year degree program will graduate within four years, and less than 60 percent will graduate within six years. Students who haven't graduated within six years probably never will.

Alex Tabarrok

Charles and I go back since college. None of us thought this would happen, we just wanted to play basketball. This is the highest honor that can ever be paid, and it's mind-blowing.

Dominique Wilkins

I was lucky enough not to face any required summer reading lists until I went to college. So I still think of summer as the best time to read for fun.

Margaret Haddix

Instead, California is one of only 10 states that provides in-state college and university tuition to illegal immigrants. That's grossly unfair to a legal high school student who moves out of California for a year, then returns to attend college.

Elton Gallegly

My father is a college professor and that's about the extent of my college experience. I'm sort of a professional student forever. I think just as human beings we always have a student who is alive in us and is waiting to pop up and make us feel like we are 16 years-old again.

Gabriel Mann

Have I ever pretended to be something? I think back in college I think I might have told a girl that I was a professional tennis player once. And then, of course, she had never heard of me so I had to dig deeper. 'I'm just sort of on the playing satellites. You know, I'm kind of working my way up. I'm not ranked in the top 100 or anything.'

James Roday

I loved 'Space Ghost' when I was in college.

Eric Andre

I grew up in a rural area. I grew up in deep southern middle Tennessee, probably about thirty miles from the Alabama border. There's nothing there, really. And the TV was my link to the outside world. It's what kept me from going into factory employment. It's what made me want to go to college. It was really inspiring.

DJ Qualls

I've met girls in college that say to me, 'Is it bad that I'm 25 and I'm in love with Ross Lynch?'

Ross Lynch

I reached a time in college when I didn't know what I wanted to do. At that time, women's careers were essentially nursing, secretarial and teaching. My mother advised me to get my teacher's certificate.

Kay Granger

My daughter just graduated college and she's a dance major. She's done a couple of dance videos already and won Miss Massachusetts a couple of weeks ago. She's going out for Miss United States the second week of July, out in Las Vegas. She will probably wind up going to New York and trying the Broadway thing.

Doug Flutie

I've always been a creative speller and never achieved good grades in school. I graduated from high school but didn't have the opportunity to attend college, so I did what young women my age did at the time - I married.

Debbie Macomber

I enjoyed mathematics from a very young age. At the beginning of college, I had this illusion, which was kind of silly in retrospect, that if I just understood math and physics and philosophy, I could figure out everything else from first principles.

Erez Lieberman Aiden

I've taken every writing class I've had available. I took classes in high school, and I took English and writing classes in community college, but I dropped out of college. I also attended a local writing workshop two years ago.

Amanda Hocking

After college, I went to Alley Theatre in Houston to work in their apprentice actor program. I thought I was gonna get discovered. It didn't happen. I moved back to Germantown, Tennessee, outside of Memphis, and taught at my old high school.

Chris Parnell

Being on a movie set when you have a great strong people there supporting you can be very nurturing. You get to explore these creative parts of yourself as a child that most people don't explore until they're in college.

Mae Whitman

For right now, I still believe that college is what's going to make me the happiest girl.

Missy Franklin

Then I left that school and I went to Cerritos College, which was in southern California; they had one of the best big band programs in the country at the time.

Bobby McFerrin

Then when I was in grammar school I played the clarinet, and then, after clarinet I played the flute in college orchestra - besides singing in the college chorus and things like that.

Bobby McFerrin

I'm a little bit of a weirdo - I'm kind of a loner, I didn't go to college, I spend a lot of my time reading. I've been working since I was 17, so that's sort of been my life.

Zosia Mamet

The acting bug just seemed to stick with me. I loved going to theatre school in college and continued to train in film classes and had been auditioning for T.V. and movie roles since I was in my late teens. My career has been slow and steady, and I kind of like it that way.

Laura Mennell

I might say that in retrospect, looking at where the community college system is today, I think we may have gone too far. The community college system is so big, so broad, so consuming of tax money.

Daniel J. Evans

I basically modeled my way through college, doing local runway shows in L.A. that don't pay a lot and a couple of shows in N.Y. and S.F., and I probably made the same as the average 19-year-old waiter; I just worked less and was around beautiful girls, so it was nice.

Mehcad Brooks

For the longest time I was afraid I'd have to keep on working at the factories. There was a steel mill and a pottery; if you didn't go to college, you went to work in those places.

Daniel Johnston

When I was in college, I had only one ambition that one day I would like to be a director.

Yash Chopra

There's definitely a world view among college students that appreciates the need to act in the international community.

Jeanne Shaheen

The role of a liberal arts college within a university is to be a genuine part of that university, giving and responding to the other parts.

Edward Levi

I do regret that when I went to college, I didn't have a liberal arts education. I got a BFA in musical theater, so it was a very directed toward what I was doing. I wish that I had expanded my horizons a little bit.

Heather Dubrow

I love puppies, and I love animals in general. Besides that, I do martial arts: extreme martial arts. I also play real guitar and drums, and sing. And I'm taking some college classes, hoping to major in English and creative writing.

Cameron Monaghan

I was dishwasher, then promoted to chef in a local kitchen in a restaurant in Seattle, and I was working on a building site as well, putting in insulation and painting houses, and then doing some classes at a community college nearby.

Alexis Denisof

I came up, I suppose, a fairly traditional way. I went to art college. I always wanted to be a stills photographer, really, when I was younger, and I briefly worked as a stills photographer.

Roger Deakins

I remember when I was in college, people told me I couldn't play in the NBA. There's always somebody saying you can't do it, and those people have to be ignored.

Bill Cartwright

I always say that I went to the College of Blossoms and the University of Ray Charles.

Merry Clayton

I started going to acting school in my senior year in high school, and I remained in acting school through four years of college.

Dane DeHaan

I dated a lot of girls all through high school, and in college I dated a young lady for about eight months.

Danny Pintauro

I grew up on a dairy farm in Southeastern Connecticut, and I went into the Peace Corps right after college. I went to

Ghana. I fell in love with Africa and have basically been working in Africa ever since.

Bruce Wilkinson

My mother keeps things in perspective for me. She makes me realize that the acting I do and love is no more important than what one of my brothers does-he works in a shoe repair shop. If my career ever tapers off, I'll go to college.

Dana Hill

We spend our spare time taking care of little things. I can watch a little bit of college and professional football if I want to... Our favorite pastime is trying to take pictures of our hometowns from space.

Kevin A. Ford

I'm not even an engineer. I don't have a college degree; I hire guys with college degrees.

Woody Norris

Folk music was out there. Clubs were springing up and they were hot with the college kids.

Dick Smothers

I even lived on campus to get the college experience. I had five roommates and I still keep in touch with them while I'm on the road.

Tatyana Ali

I went into broadcast journalism. I loved every class I took, I just got anxious because I came to the realization that you're groomed in high school to get good SAT scores to get into a good college or else you're done for.

Chace Crawford

I was a baseball player. I played in high school and a little bit in college. I was a catcher. I don't know if I could have played any other position. As a catcher, you're always on the ball.

Tim DeKay

I went to art school in Chicago for a year at Columbia College. I had this whole master plan of getting into sustainable development and green architecture and construction, so I wanted to go to business school and then get my masters in construction and development.

Nico Tortorella

Throughout my college years, I'd watch my sister squeal every Christmas as she unwrapped another 'Buffy' DVD set. I didn't know much about the series, but I was filled with that obnoxious self-importance that comes from having decided to be an Academic Who Reads Serious Things.

Marie Rutkoski

You gotta understand, there are two different kinds of Asians - the kind who are good at school, obey their parents, go to college - that kind of stuff. And then you have my family - me, my brother, all of my cousins - we're just wretched people.

Bobby Lee

I graduated from college in Ohio and bummed around for a while, and then I joined VISTA, which was a domestic Peace Corps kind of thing, and they sent me to Colorado.

Mojo Nixon

It's a tough life being a pop star. You know, at the end of the day when you've paid all the bills and put the kids through college and that, you know, there's only enough left for a small island off the South Pacific.

Larry Mullen

I've learned a lot from the experiences that I went through in high school, through college and overseas, and just everything in life. That is what prepared me for coming into the NBA, being undersized, no recognition, not getting anything easy, and I have been fortunate to prosper in this league.

Udonis Haslem

Everyone, whether you are married or have a boyfriend or girlfriend, there's always someone who has a hold of your heart. You learn to let it go, but there's always a place in your heart. For me, it was someone I went to college with and we had an amazing bond, but I left.

Kip Moore

I enjoy listening to contemporary rock on the college stations while I'm taking long walks, love gospel and soul music, am fascinated by hip-hop and rap as the new kind of urban 'beat' poetry and, come to think of it, find something interesting about just any kind of music.

Oscar Hijuelos

We have such a high drop-out rate from musicians, said the head of the college. He was right - I dropped out before I even dropped in. Months later they were still asking what had happened to me, not realising that I was on a UK tour.

Holly Johnson

I was resolved to sustain and preserve in my college the bite of the mind, the chance to stand face to face with truth, the good life lived in a small, various, highly articulate and democratic society.

Virginia Gildersleeve

On paper, actors are the dumbest group of individuals essentially out there. Most of us have not gone to college. However, we never stop learning. Because of what we do, we're constantly researching, constantly learning.

Mike Vogel

I wasn't really driven to be an actor or anything, but in college I decided to study acting, much to my parents' disappointment. I attended Mason Gross School of the Arts at Rutgers where Bill Esper was, and that is where I really got hooked on the art of acting, and, almost, the chemistry of acting.

Roger Bart

You come for the money, you don't come to Barefoot College. You come for the work and the challenge, you'll come to the Barefoot College. That is where we want you to try crazy ideas. Whatever idea you have, come and try it. It doesn't matter if you fail. Battered, bruised, you start again.

Bunker Roy

You have to be a cop-out or a wash-out or a dropout to come to our college. You have to work with your hands. You have to have a dignity of labor. You have to show that you have a skill that you can offer to the community and provide a service to the community. So we started the Barefoot College, and we redefined professionalism.

Bunker Roy

Before college, I acted in my room, to classical music, because music tells stories. I'd put on a record and proceed, silently. I'd keep putting the needle back to a certain segment because I hadn't died well enough. I had to really, really feel dead. I'd love to do a death scene.

Amanda Plummer

If I can't act, I would go to college and maybe be a veterinarian.

Megan Charpentier

Middle class families are struggling to send their sons and daughters to school. For many Americans, a college education is essential to future success.

Albio Sires

I never went to college when I was young and am looking forward to giving it a try... at age 65!

Martin Sheen

After I'd been in college for a couple years I'd read Shakespeare and Frost and Chaucer and the poets of the Harlem Renaissance. I'd come to appreciate how gorgeous the English language could be. But most fantasy novels didn't seem to make the effort.

Patrick Rothfuss

Presidents are elected not by direct popular vote but by 538 members of the Electoral College.

Thomas E. Mann

When I was 15 years old and in the tenth grade, I heard of Martin Luther King, Jr. Three years later, when I was 18, I met Dr. King and we became friends. Two years after that I became very involved in the civil rights movement. I was in college at that time. As I got more and more involved, I saw politics as a means of bringing about change.

John Lewis

Much as banks don't care where your money's coming from, the Electoral College is all 'don't ask, don't care' when it comes to votes.

John Ridley

America is the student who defies the odds to become the first in a family to go to college - the citizen who defies the cynics and goes out there and votes - the young person who comes out of the shadows to demand the right to dream. That's what America is about.

Barack Obama

The Christian fact is very straightforward: To be a student is a calling. Your parents are setting up accounts to pay the bills, or you are scraping together your own resources and taking out loans, or a scholarship is making college possible.

Stanley Hauerwas

You have young men of color in many communities who are more likely to end up in jail or in the criminal justice system than they are in a good job or in college. And, you know, part of my job, that I can do, I think, without any potential conflicts, is to get at those root causes.

Barack Obama

Before the 1970s, banks were banks. They did what banks were supposed to do in a state capitalist economy: they took unused funds from your bank account, for example, and transferred them to some potentially useful purpose like helping a family buy a home or send a kid to college.

Noam Chomsky

I got my diploma from Ealing College of Art, in graphics and illustration.

Freddie Mercury

A university is what a college becomes when the faculty loses interest in the students.

John Ciardi

I've been composing music all my life and if I'd been clever enough at school I would like to have gone to music college.

Anthony Hopkins

I just wanted to be a composer; I became an actor by default, really. I got a scholarship to a college of music and drama, hoping to take a scholarship in music. But I ended up as an acting student, so I've stuck with that for the last 50-odd years.

Anthony Hopkins

I don't think college wrestling is in danger of extinction by any means. But I am concerned if one program drops.

Dan Gable

I want to go to college. I'm going to take four years off. I don't want to miss that. I want to be a writer. I think that'd be awesome.

Kristen Stewart

I was born in the U.S., my wife was born in Mexico and emigrated here when she was in college, and my daughters were born in New York City. That makes them passport-carrying, natural-born, eligible-to-run-for-president Americans. But they're also Mexicans and they like that just fine.

Jeffrey Kluger

I have a daughter who is a sophomore in college and another who is in the 11th grade of high school.

Thomas Friedman

I left home to go to college, and then I moved back home. I moved back for three years from 21 to 24.

Will Ferrell

I have always had the feeling I could do anything and my dad told me I could. I was in college before I found out he might be wrong.

Ann Richards

And sex is definitely part of college life.

Scott Speedman

I really wanted to be a doctor, until my freshman year of college when I realized that while I was good at chemistry and biology, I really wasn't feeling challenged by it.

Marissa Mayer

Where I grew up in Dallas, things might be a little more traditional. People have the same things in mind. They're supposed to grow up, go to college, get a job, get married, and have children, grandchildren. That's the world I grew up in.

Lisa Loeb

College ain't so much where you been as how you talk when you get back.

Ossie Davis

I did a lot of theater when I was in high school and college. I also did stand-up in college, so it was always part of what I did.

Seth MacFarlane

After high school, I enrolled at the University of Nebraska at Lincoln, but I stayed only a year and a half. I felt college was a waste of time; I wanted to start working.

Evan Williams

My parents were not affluent people and were not - didn't come from the extremities of education. My mother had a high school diploma. I often think I so wish she'd come out of the hills in Appalachia and been able to go on to college. I think she would have made a wonderful teacher.

Dwight Yoakam

There's far more that goes into being a professional athlete than being a college athlete. So many differences that people don't realize. It's not just about playing football and getting paid to do it. There's a lot of things that you have to deal with.

Robert Griffin III

That's another piece of advice: Don't go to college; follow your dreams. Unless you're a doctor - then go to college.

Adam DeVine

It's clear enough that there was substantial fraud in Ohio, thus delivering the Electoral College vote for President Bush.

George Galloway

Athletes who take to the classroom naturally or are encouraged to focus on grades should be able to do well in the classroom. I believe the reason you go to college is to get your degree. It's not a minor league or an audition for the pros.

Rebecca Lobo

Going back to high school and college, I believed I would be involved in public service. I literally could not conceptualize anything else.

Bill de Blasio

My first job was working at Benihana as kitchen help. In college, I was a telemarketer for a company at the same time I was a bike messenger for this greasy fast-food place.

Steve Aoki

I often have said that to be a college president, you need a thick skin, a good sense of humor, and nerves like sewer pipes.

Gordon Gee

Education is a private matter between the person and the world of knowledge and experience, and has little to do with school or college.

Lillian Smith

After college, I was living in New York and wrote furiously, a huge novel that I knew was a failure. I hoped that the book would work, but to be honest, I think I knew it would never work, even as I was finishing it.

Chang-Rae Lee

When I entered college, it was to study liberal arts. At the University of Pennsylvania, I studied English literature, but I fell in love with broadcasting, with telling stories about other people's exploits.

Andrea Mitchell

Many students graduate from college and professional schools, including those of social work, nursing, medicine, teaching and law, with crushing debt burdens.

Jon Porter

College graduates work in every sector of the American economy, and the research engines incubated within our universities generate a wealth of ideas and innovations that have an enormous impact on our lives.

Gordon Gee

With the draft, everybody was involved. Everybody was fodder. When you got to be 21, 22 and graduated from college, for two years your life stopped. If you had been running in the direction of your life, you had to stop and do this other thing which was, if not menacing, just plain boring.

Philip Roth

I'm in Delta Delta Delta, otherwise known as Tri-Delta. I've developed some great friendships, and it's enabled me to have a little bit more of a normal college experience.

Meryl Davis

My co-founder Dylan Smith and I left our junior year of college to move to the Bay Area. To the horror of our friends' parents, we actually had two other friends drop out of college to work on the product. The four of us were just working non-stop growing Box.

Aaron Levie

At Gallaudet, deafness isn't an issue. You don't even think about it. Students can pay attention to accounting or psychology or journalism. But when a deaf person goes to another college, no matter how supportive it is, that person doesn't get the same access.

I. King Jordan

I did not take a calculus course until my second year of college.

Robert Coleman Richardson

I always knew when I graduated from high school, I'd go to college. I never thought about what I was walking away from... I just wanted to study literature and writing.

Gaby Hoffmann

I'd started acting as a child. But I wanted to see if it was something my true personality was interested in. I stepped away from offers when I took five years off to go to college. I've only really just decided to whole-heartedly embrace acting.

Gaby Hoffmann

Liberals have invented whole college majors - psychology, sociology and women's studies - to prove that nothing is anybody's fault.

P. J. O'Rourke

Earnestness is stupidity sent to college.

P. J. O'Rourke

College professors used to be badly paid and worth it.
Colleges used to be modest institutions; they should go
back to being modest institutions.

P. J. O'Rourke

In my bright, utopian future world, they will hand out
college educations like cups of water at the end of the L.A.
Marathon.

Henry Rollins

If you don't give your kid freedom to make choices with
money, including stupid choices, he'll make plenty when he
gets to college.

John W. Gardner

I did all the musicals in my high school; I was in a pop group signed to Cash Money Records in college. Music has always been a really big part of my life.

Janina Gavankar

The only difference between your local college and a Christian seminary is that the latter is more honest.

Dennis Prager

I have a few uniforms - depending on whether I'm going to a college campus or meeting a head of state. But clean and easy works best for me.

Nancy Pelosi

My father was in Congress when I was born. He was mayor my whole life from when I was in grade school - first grade - to when I went away to college.

Nancy Pelosi

A whale ship was my Yale College and my Harvard.

Herman Melville

Most women are not programmed to prefer a great career to a great man and a family. They feel they were sold a bill of goods at college and by the media.

Dennis Prager

For seven years after college, I was a waitress at the Buttercup Bakery in Berkeley, and from there I got a job at Merrill Lynch as an account executive, from where I went to vice president of investments for Prudential-Bache Securities. I started my own firm in 1987.

Suze Orman

If you're smart enough to go to college, you should be smart and creative enough to pay for it.

Jesse Ventura

I was a scholarship minor public school day boy at Ardingly College and later Whitgift School. Then, straight into work as a journalist - a wonderful thing for a writer.

Neil Gaiman

I went to college for four years.

Kim Kardashian

Economists report that a college education adds many thousands of dollars to a man's lifetime income - which he then spends sending his son to college.

Bill Vaughan

The ideal college is Mark Hopkins on one end of a log and a student on the other.

James A. Garfield

I was sitting on the bus, and the sign said if you're ready to better your life, come to Medgar Evers College, and I got off the bus and went to Medgar Evers College.

Iyanla Vanzant

Michael Jordan and Magic and myself all learned how to play the game in college programs that emphasized the team.

Kareem Abdul-Jabbar

So somebody told me that if I wasn't a coffee drinker yet, by the end of college I'd have to be, because a math major is so tough I would have to stay up very late. I was going to need coffee to do that. Well, merely because they said that, I never drank coffee in college, never got addicted to it, never needed it.

Danica McKellar

How you play the game is for college ball. When you're playing for money, winning is the only thing that matters.

Leo Durocher

I didn't really decide that I wanted to be an astronaut for sure until the end of college.

Sally Ride

I loved teaching and I did a lot of work as a teacher's assistant in college, and my favorite experience was basically getting a laugh from a bunch of people because they had just understood something.

Joss Whedon

I never took classic business classes in college, so I don't have the background that any of the people running large companies have.

Howard Schultz

I don't see kids with Palm Pilots. They are not common on college campuses, except among professors. Gen Xers don't need them. They are a phenomenon of the 50-something who can't remember if his broker's number ends in 1137 or 3317.

Elliott Abrams

I wanted to be a genetic engineer. That was my goal in college. I wanted to figure out what the codon sequence was that causes replication in a cardio myopathic virus. That was my goal.

Ashton Kutcher

The same independence that got me into trouble in high school got me praise in college.

Alan Dershowitz

My parents started with very little and were the only ones in their families to graduate from college. As parents, they focused on education, but did not stop at academics - they made sure that we knew music, saw art and theatre and traveled - even though it meant budgeting like crazy.

Jennifer Garner

An awful lot of people come to college with this strange idea that there's no longer segregation in America's schools, that our schools are basically equal; neither of these things is true.

Jonathan Kozol

All through college, I had frequently been the only girl in a science class - which wasn't such a bad deal.

Sylvia Earle

Back in the 1960s , I got a superb education for very little money. The bill for my first year at Harpur College in New York was a few hundred dollars.

Camille Paglia

I never had a strategy about my life. I didn't have enough information to have a strategy. I'm the first person in my family to go to college. I had no family mentors.

Alan Dershowitz

Don't ever dare to take your college as a matter of course - because, like democracy and freedom, many people you'll never know have broken their hearts to get it for you.

Alice Miller

So I decided on science when I was in college.

Sally Ride

In my case, I was born to parents who were very young, and I don't think they were entirely ready to have a child. My dad was going to college and working two or three jobs at the same time, and my mum was working and going to school.

Gillian Anderson

When it comes to college education, American families are paying more and getting less.

Patricia Schroeder

At the risk of being forgotten completely by the media, I went to college and pursued a passion that had nothing to do with acting: mathematics.

Danica McKellar

I took a public speaking class in college and managed to make the class laugh a little bit.

Kevin James

College campuses were once a hotbed of political activity.

Tom Ford

I conceived in art college at the age of 20, near the end of term.

Joni Mitchell

I was a short order cook in a pool hall in college. So, I am the fastest cook in the world.

Sharon Stone

My parents were disappointed I didn't finish college, and they were really upset when I went to Hollywood to become an actor. I was a big disappointment to them.

George Clooney

We all need to save money to send our kids to college, to buy our first house, and to retire. But the truth is that most of us don't save very much.

Timothy Noah

When I was in college, I wanted to write for 'Late Night With Conan O'Brien,' and I was an intern there.

Mike Birbiglia

Almost every time I am in a lectureship on a college campus, young people will say, If there is a God and if he is a loving and merciful God, how do you explain the problems of suffering and death and all the tragedies that happen to people?

John Clayton

I believe in research. Each movie at Pixar involves research with college professors or taking trips to learn as much as we can about a particular subject matter.

John Lasseter

The professional world was much more unpleasant than I thought. I was always wishing I could get back that enthusiasm I had when I was doing shows at college.

Francis Ford Coppola

I met someone the other night who's 28 years old, and he hasn't worked a day since he left college because he's pursuing a dream he'll never, ever realize: He thinks he's a great singer. Actually, he's crap.

Simon Cowell

In college, you learn how to learn. Four years is not too much time to spend at that.

Mary Oliver

But boxing was my profession. I had to go back the second time because I was broke and I couldn't just go and get a college degree and earn it. I had too many bills, too many families.

George Foreman

When Americans think of college these days, the first word that often comes to mind is 'debt.' And from 'debt' it's just a short hop to other unpleasant words, like 'payola,' 'kickback,' and 'bribery.'

James Surowiecki

I never went to college - I barely got out of high school.

Dave Matthews

I'm fortunate now that I coach at Duke University and we've won a lot. I have some kids who haven't failed that much. But when they get to college, they're going to fail some time. That's a thing that I can help them the most with.

Mike Krzyzewski

When I was younger, I was a complete tomboy. Then in college I started emerging out of the tomboy stage and dressing differently.

Hope Solo

College was just so essential for my sense of self and my development.

Claire Danes

I am often amazed at how much more capability and enthusiasm for science there is among elementary school youngsters than among college students.

Carl Sagan

All my friends were in college when I was making 'Superbad.' We were drinking beer and watching movies and eating pizza. It wasn't like I was going to nice restaurants or anything like that, and I lived like a frat guy. Eventually it was time to grow up, be healthy and be responsible. You can't live like a kid forever, you know?

Jonah Hill

That's the value of a college education... I don't know anywhere in the world where you can make an investment and make that kind of return.

Gaston Caperton

There are no college courses to build up self-esteem or high school or elementary school. If you don't get those values at a early age, nurtured in your home, you don't get them.

T. D. Jakes

It is not so important to be serious as it is to be serious about the important things. The monkey wears an expression of seriousness which would do credit to any college student, but the monkey is serious because he itches.

Robert M. Hutchins

Community colleges are one of America's great social inventions a gateway to the future for first time students looking for an affordable college education, and for mid-career students looking to get ahead in the workplace.

Barbara Mikulski

Jazz is the big brother of the blues. If a guy's playing blues like we play, he's in high school. When he starts playing jazz it's like going on to college, to a school of higher learning.

B. B. King

The most experience I had in the criminology field is playing a thug as an actor. That was my first paid job. The police academy at the college was paying people to reenact the calls that potential cops would get. So I got to play thugs and people who were unruly.

Jeremy Renner

I'm here not just as an actress but as a woman, an African-American, a granddaughter of Ellis Island immigrants, a person who could not have afforded college without the help of student loans and as one of millions of volunteers working to re-elect President Obama!

Kerry Washington

I could describe my career in two words: who knew. I was on the path to becoming a professional baseball player, but I got injured in college. When I decided to move out to L.A. to try acting, nobody was betting on me, not even my family. But it's always been that way for me; nothing has come easy.

Shemar Moore

I didn't have good grades until I started dancing, because I didn't try - I didn't see the point. Once I realized why I wanted to go to college, I started to study and do well. I knew I had to have a certain GPA to get in.

Kyle Abraham

I wrote my thesis on the benefits of war and very near got thrown out of college. But I can show you where the greatest advancement of mankind comes under stress and strain, not comfort.

Don Young

When I wrote 'The World Is Flat,' I said the world is flat. Yeah, we're all connected. Facebook didn't exist; Twitter was a sound; the cloud was in the sky; 4G was a parking place; LinkedIn was a prison; applications were what you sent to college; and Skype, for most people, was a typo.

Thomas Friedman

I grew up below the poverty line; I didn't have as much as other people did. I think it made me stronger as a person, it built my character. Now I have a 4.0 grade point average and I want to go to college, and just become a better person.

Justin Bieber

Major League Baseball has the best idea of all. Three years before they'll take a kid out of college, then they have a minor league system that they put the kids in. I'm sure that if the NBA followed the same thing, there would be a lot of kids in a minor league system that still were not good enough to play in the major NBA.

Bobby Knight

And affirmative action is a very nice term for racial discrimination against better-qualified white people in jobs, employment, promotions and scholarships, and college admittance.

David Duke

I learned law so well, the day I graduated I sued the college, won the case, and got my tuition back.

Fred Allen

I believe God wants you to have money to pay your bills, send your kids to college and do charity work and build orphanages. There's the teaching that we're supposed to be poor to show that we're humble. I don't buy that. I think we're supposed to be leaders. We're supposed to excel.

Joel Osteen

I always just forced myself to do crazy things in public. In college I would push an overhead projector across campus with my pants just low enough to show my butt. Then my friend would incite the crowd to be like, 'Look at that idiot!' That's how I got over being shy.

Will Ferrell

I prefer ordinary girls - you know, college students, waitresses, that sort of thing. Most of the girls I go out with are just good friends. Just because I go out to the cinema with a girl, it doesn't mean we are dating.

Leonardo DiCaprio

I wouldn't want to go back over my life. I've done it all. I wouldn't have wanted to miss the Marine Corps. I wouldn't have wanted to miss the war. I wouldn't have missed college. Or playin' for the Colts. I got all the money I need. Five children. I got a truck. I have no regrets whatsoever.

Art Donovan

Like anyone who goes to college, you're leaving a familiar surrounding and a comfortable environment and your friends and everything, and you're starting fresh. It can be pretty daunting.

Jason Biggs

People of my age who went to college, go into college, you know what it cost back then? Nothing or next to nothing. At the most, you had to work at Dairy Queen during the summer and that would pay for your college education.

Michael Moore

Many kids come out of college, they have a credit card and a diploma. They don't know how to buy a house or a car or health insurance or life insurance. They do not know basic microeconomics.

Jesse Jackson

When I look back over my life it's almost as if there was a plan laid out for me - from the little girl who was so passionate about animals who longed to go to Africa and whose family couldn't afford to put her through college.

Everyone laughed at my dreams. I was supposed to be a secretary in Bournemouth.

Jane Goodall

Bankruptcy laws allow companies to smoothly reorganize, but not college graduates burdened by student loans.

Robert Reich

Willie Mays was the best ever. When I was in college I once made a catch like the one Mays made over his head. Sometimes when I'm lying in bed at night I think about it. It still makes me warm.

David Duchovny

There's a picture of my dorm room in the college yearbook as the most messy, most disgusting room on the Harvard campus, where I was an undergraduate.

Brian Greene

The college stations have a big voice, and I would like to become more involved with them. I would like to have symposiums with the members of various college radio stations.

Angie Stone

Going to college and studying music is not a bad idea at all. I don't know if you can go to college and be taught heart.

Blake Shelton

I used to write a lot of songs. I was an English major in college. I was a deluded poet for a year. Totally deluded.

Paul Dano

I was sort of shocked when it all of a sudden turned out that I got all A's through college, with the exception of two B's in the first term. I never envisaged myself as summa cum laude.

Alan Greenspan

I always give the example, if you turn on the radio today, black radio, Lenny Kravitz is not black. Bob Marley wasn't black: in the beginning, only white college stations played Bob Marley.

Spike Lee

You know that it is only through work that you can achieve anything, either in college or in the world.

Charles William Eliot

I love the idea of going to work and having to fight and learn a new skill set, whether it's muay Thai or Kali or Filipino stick fighting. To me, it's like college for life.

Jeremy Renner

I can remember, when I was in college, irritating deeply somebody I was going out with, because he would ask me what I was thinking and I would say I was thinking nothing. And it was true.

Joan Didion

I had a difficult time hearing my own inner voice about what I wanted to be in this life, because there were all these perfect examples of what a man actually does. The notion is that he goes to college, gets married and provides. That's what a man does.

Kevin Costner

My college degree was in theater. But the real reason, if I have any success in that milieu, so to speak, is because I spent a lot of years directing, I spent a lot of years behind the camera.

Alton Brown

I grew up in the inner city of Chicago, and then I moved to Robbins, and it kind of raised me. When I was in college, I actually had them change the starting lineup to say 'from Robbins, Illinois' instead of 'Chicago, Illinois.'

Dwyane Wade

I discovered Christopher Isherwood in college. His writing style is so direct, warm, and inclusive.

Claire Danes

I spent a college semester in a small town in Italy - and that is where I truly tasted food for the first time.

Alton Brown

When I graduated from college in the spring of 1970, I decided to hitchhike around Europe with my guitar and my backpack. I was gone for about four months.

John Oates

In many of the high schools in the South Bronx, more children will end up in prison than will go to college.

Jonathan Kozol

Everyone is taught the essentials of writing for at least 13 years, maybe more if they go to college. Nobody is taught music or tap dancing that way.

Tom Wolfe

I worked at a hospital for a week. And at a golf course when I was in college at Kansas for about a week. The tips weren't good so I quit.

Paul Pierce

I can't read music. Instead, I'd do stuff inside the piano, do harmonics and all kinds of crazy things. They used to put me in these annual piano contests down at Long Beach City College, and two years in a row, I won first prize - out of like 5,000 kids!

Eddie Van Halen

I kicked college nostalgia in my late 20s. As much as I loved college and treasure the memories, I no longer want to go back.

Josh Radnor

Instead of going to college, I spent my time out on the road learning how to be a better musician.

Miranda Lambert

I wanted to go to a liberal arts college, I wanted to have that experience.

Mandy Patinkin

I wanted to go to a good college, and my mind was set on Wellesley.

Marjory Stoneman Douglas

In real life, I first started sleep walking in high school because that was when this concept of getting into college first appeared. I had this moment of, 'Oh! This is going to affect the rest of my life.'

Mike Birbiglia

In college, you're kind of designing who you want to be. And I wanted to be a big reader.

Josh Radnor

I didn't care for most of the books I was being asked to read in school. I started reading like crazy right after high school when I got a job in a mental hospital. I was working my way through college, and I did a lot of night shifts, and there was nothing to do. So I read like crazy, serious stuff, all the classics.

James Patterson

I wanted to win the gold medal and then go home and further my education in college. I had no intentions whatsoever to become a professional fighter because I had heard horror stories about former boxers who made money but, in the end, ended up with nothing. I didn't want to be one of those guys.

Sugar Ray Leonard

I was an economics major in college, and every summer after school, I would drive my car from California, from Claremont men's college at the time, to New York. And I worked on Wall Street.

Henry Kravis

'CSI' has not only remained a top-rated show through seven seasons; it has had real-world consequences. Police and prosecutors complain of a "CSI' effect' that leads juries to demand more physical evidence than they used to expect. College officials use the same term to describe spiking enrollment in forensic-science programs.

Virginia Postrel

From its humble origins in college dorm rooms, social media has quietly crept into the boardroom.

Ryan Holmes

The first dream I had was just to get a college education. I got through college in three years, taking extra classes in summer school.

Eli Broad

I love the idea that we put in jokes the kids don't get. And that later, when they grow up and read a few books and go to college and watch the show again, they can get it on a completely different level.

Matt Groening

When I started Netscape I was brand new out of college and all the aspects of building a business, like balance sheets and hiring people, were new to me.

Marc Andreessen

On the day I started college in 1979, no woman had ever been on the United States Supreme Court or served as the Speaker of the House. None had been an astronaut or the solo anchor of a network evening news broadcast. Not one had been president of an Ivy League college or run a serious campaign for president.

Dee Dee Myers

I majored in English in college, so I read the classic dystopian novels like '1984' and 'Brave New World.'

Lois Lowry

I went to school, I went to college. I know how to read. Even though I lack common sense sometimes, I am book smart.

Nicole Polizzi

Borrowing to pay for college used to be the exception; now it's the rule.

Arne Duncan

Not graduating high school on time leads to fewer chances of attending college and obtaining good paying jobs, and creates instead higher chances of incarceration and unemployment.

Al Sharpton

I want to go to college and go back to Georgetown. It's a really cool place.

Bobby Flay

Public education must be viewed from the lens of providing each child with the learning environment that best meets his or her needs. If we can send a low-income child to a parochial school, knowing that his odds of attending college will increase as a result, then that should be our mission.

Jeb Bush

I've been a Mac guy for almost my entire adult life. I wrote my first college papers on a typewriter, but by the end of my freshman year - almost 20 years ago - I was on an IBM PC. Then, in 1984, I found the Mac, and I never looked back.

John Battelle

A college education shows a man how little other people know.

Thomas Chandler Haliburton

I joined the Madras Christian College but dropped out after three months. Telugu music director Ramesh Naidu asked me to assist him, and I did so for over a year. I did think of rejoining college, but by then, I was discovering the musician in me. I worked with Illaya Raja and Raj Koti and soon shifted to commercials. This led to movie offers.

A. R. Rahman

I can see a day soon where you'll create your own college degree by taking the best online courses from the best professors from around the world - some computing from Stanford, some entrepreneurship from Wharton, some ethics from Brandeis, some literature from Edinburgh - paying only the nominal fee for the certificates of completion.

Thomas Friedman

I'm a lesbian. Yup. Hundred percent. Hundred percent. I remember being in college, and I had fallen in love with this woman, and I remember sitting in my dorm room saying out loud to myself, like, 'You have enough problems. You are not gonna let this happen.'

Christine Quinn

My first college roommate greeted me with a shocked silence followed by, 'So... you're black.'

Al Roker

In a world of deep injustice and violence, a people exists that thinks some can be given time to study. We need you to take seriously the calling that is yours by virtue of going to college.

Stanley Hauerwas

It's unexpected for women's issues to be brought up in places other than women's centers on college campuses or crisis places.

Kathleen Hanna

Pizza made me who I am. In the summer of 1998, I dropped out of college and started a pizza restaurant called Growlies in my hometown in rural Canada. My seed money: a credit card with a $20,000 limit.

Ryan Holmes

The world I live in is benefiting from things like satellite radio. Jazz and blues fests are everywhere now, and Americana is going strong on college radio. What I'm hearing is an appreciation of real music.

Bonnie Raitt

A president, like a college freshman, can't know in advance which questions he'll have to answer or what topics he'll have to master. He has to be flexible, supple, and responsive. He has to be comfortable with multiple-choice.

Walter Kirn

I think it's sort of an outrage that companies should have to hire firms to teach the college graduates they employ how to write.

Derek Bok

I remember those days right after I graduated from college. All I had to do was wake up in the morning and think about writing songs. It's not like that anymore, needless to say.

Josh Turner

I wanted to be a classical actress. I plodded along. I went to junior college in San Francisco, I was in a Repertory Company. My hero was Eva Le Gallienne, who was a great theater actress at the turn of the century who created her own company, and she wrote these hilarious autobiographies at the time.

Annette Bening

Stay in college, kids. Otherwise, you may become an umpire.

Andy Roddick

Once I started down the path of co-founding Image Comics, and even co-publisher, it just seems a lot more like a career path that isn't that atypical for someone with a college degree. Whereas, someone who draws comic books as a freelancer and lives from job to job is a more unusual story.

Jim Lee

It was 1999, and we were building a way for college kids to create online profiles for the purpose of sharing... with employers. Oops. I vividly remember the moment I realized my company was going to fail. My co-founder and I were at our wits' end. By 2001, the dot-com bubble had burst, and we had spent all our money.

Eric Ries

I suggest that the introductory courses in science, at all levels from grade school through college, be radically revised. Leave the fundamentals, the so-called basics, aside for a while, and concentrate the attention of all students on the things that are not known.

Lewis Thomas

Ever since college, I have been a libertarian - socially liberal and fiscally conservative. I believe in individual liberty and personal responsibility.

Michael Shermer

Friends of friends had bands in college or in their early 20s and had a moment where they had some kind of interest from a record label or manager. It's always interesting how people handle those decisions and those moments.

Noah Baumbach

It seems everyone knows a college degree is important, but few have a plan to keep it affordable.

LZ Granderson

There are something like 300 anti-genocide chapters on college campuses around the country. It's bigger than the anti-apartheid movement. There are something like 500 high school chapters devoted to stopping the genocide in Darfur. Evangelicals have joined it. Jewish groups have joined it.

Samantha Power

We, after a certain age, after college, are so consumed about what we want to achieve in life, and we fiercely are ambitious and we go after that, but sometimes we tend to take all our loved and dear ones for granted.

Ranbir Kapoor

I did once shatter a chandelier. I was singing with my college choir in Wales. I was the soloist and I hit the high note and there was this massive bang and all this glass came down from the ceiling. I'd like that to be my party trick if I can perfect it.

Katherine Jenkins

And my father didn't have money for me to go to college. And at that particular time they didn't have black quarterbacks, and I don't think I could have made it in basketball, because I was only 5' 11". So I just picked baseball.

Willie Mays

As much as I'd like to think and as much as people mistakenly think my audience is blue collar people in the heart of America, my audience is basically, in the States, an NPR audience. I play college towns in the summer because that's who comes to see me.

Steve Earle

The most frequent complaint I hear from college students is that professors inject their leftist political comments into their courses even when they have nothing to do with the subject.

Phyllis Schlafly

Pick up any newspaper in the morning. Count the words in the lead sentences. There will be at least 25 in all of them: Guaranteed. The writers just want to tell you how many degrees they have from this college or that university.

Jimmy Breslin

Your son and your daughter needs an excellent father more than an excellent college.

Nick Vujicic

I am a firm believer in education and have worked very hard to tell young Latinos that they must go to college and that, if possible, they should pursue an advanced degree. I am convinced that education is the great equalizer.

Jimmy Smits

It takes most men five years to recover from a college education, and to learn that poetry is as vital to thinking as knowledge.

Brooks Atkinson

I'm a big sports fan. College football is my favorite.

Verne Troyer

Without any formal personal finance instruction in our high school or college curricula, many college seniors who graduate in the red will continue to make common financial mistakes that only exacerbate their debt burdens.

Alexa Von Tobel

When I was in college, my parents' house burned down, and took a lot of the possessions I'd grown up with. That's probably one thing that made me realize material stuff is not really that important.

Rick Riordan

So I was determined to use my last two years in college doing something I thought I would enjoy, which was acting. And it was probably because there was girls over in the drama school too, you know?

James Earl Jones

I wasn't a smart kid and I still don't think I'm too smart when it comes to book smart, but I was very good with what I knew and with my craft and I think that was my calling in life. But even today I never went to college.

Criss Angel

I have a very broad demographic, from the 8-year-old who knows every word to 'Ice Ice Baby' and the college kid who grew up on 'Ninja Rap' to the soccer mom and grandparent.

Vanilla Ice

I never did anything else. In college I switched majors every two weeks, and acting was the only thing that held my interest.

James Caan

I just developed my act way back in the late '80s. I went to college in Georgia, so I picked up the Southern accent. I talked like that with my friends all the time, because it was fun. It was funny... All my friends were real Southern. We're buddies, so I'd say stuff to make them laugh. So that was pretty much it.

Larry the Cable Guy

My problem with the wedding industry started when I studied in college and liked to have the television on in the background, and 'A Wedding Story' on TLC always came on, and I'd get irritated that the story of two people making a lifelong commitment to each other could be encapsulated in a half-hour show about the party they throw.

Jessica Valenti

I'm the first person in my family to go to college.

Jessica Chastain

When I grew up there was no web, blogging or tweeting. In fact, where I grew up there was not even television! I met a lot of my friends in school and in college, and they are still my friends today.

Indra Nooyi

I got my Bachelor's degree in nursing and worked nine years - even taught nursing in a college - before I stopped and said to myself, 'This is not who I am. I am not really a nurse inside. I'm a writer.'

Sue Monk Kidd

I remember one time being told I could not play in a basketball game at the College of William and Mary because I was black, even though I was playing with a United States Army team.

Walter Dean Myers

I can remember at college, living on 30-cent meals.

Sargent Shriver

I worked my butt off in high school and received a lot of scholarships for college and to throw all that away for acting was tough for my family, but it was just something I felt my heart pulling me towards and don't regret a single minute of it. I love to act!

Kellan Lutz

When I was at college, I worked in a department store called Brit Home Stores, which is a pretty lackluster department store, selling clothes for middle-aged women. My job was to walk the floor and find anything that was damaged, take it to the store room and log it.

Dominic Monaghan

I went to college at the University of Kansas, where I got a degree in political science.

Sara Paretsky

To me, all writing is like music. And especially dialogue. I studied music in college; that is what I wanted to be, a composer. Acting got me sidetracked.

Dirk Benedict

After college, I wanted to learned about myself as an American, so I left the United States and went to Japan.

Bruce Feiler

Even though I am very tied to and close to my heritage, I learned Spanish in college; I didn't grow up with it. Growing up in South Texas is different from Miami or L.A. where it is a necessity to speak Spanish.

Eva Longoria

My parents are both college professors, and it made me want to question authority, standards and traditions.

Maya Lin

There are many reasons why I hate college football. The 4-hour games drone on longer than Steve Lyons during the American League playoffs. The ever-expanding season threatens to creep into early July. Boise, Idaho, hosts a bowl game. And it's played on blue artificial turf.

Stephen Rodrick

Texas is now a cornerstone of the electoral college for Republicans.

Ed Gillespie

My parents did a great job raising me and my two sisters. We all graduated from high school and we all graduated from college. So, to be a good representative of my family is probably my greatest accomplishment thus far.

Robert Griffin III

I was lucky enough to co-found a business in college that ended up with 400 employees, and I launched 20 different projects while I was there - a project a week.

Seth Godin

They were often the first students in their family to go to college and the very idea of higher education was still foreign to them. They had to make a conscious and often difficult decision to come to college.

Michael N. Castle

When I went to college, I discovered the Sega console, and 'Sonic the Hedgehog' became very dear to me.

Edgar Wright

I discovered in college that country music could be fun adding some swing to it.

George Strait

The vast majority of students probably emerge from college with an adequate grasp of no more than a single method of inquiry. Even this capacity may erode over time if it does not relate to experiences and problems that recur in the student's later life.

Derek Bok

Economists actually disagree about whether there are significant economic returns from attending an elite college versus a less-selective one.

Emily Oster

I did have a falsetto, but I only used it when I was joking around with friends or to annoy my girlfriends, or in the shower, because no one else was around. Or in college. I'd go to karaoke bars and sing Tina Turner songs in the original key.

John Lloyd Young

I was never really interested in studies and was hot-headed and rebellious in college, as I was totally confused and insecure but was not coming to terms with it.

Emraan Hashmi

In middle school, I started to draw, and my pencil sketches were huge. They were these 4ft by 3ft drawings, and I got a lot of attention for that, so that was very validating. But I didn't start cartooning until I was in college.

Jeff Kinney

Grover Washington was my main influence, and when I went to college, I started listening to more of the jazz masters like Sonny Rollins, Cannonball Adderley, and John Coltrane.

Kenny G

When I arrived in America, I experienced serious culture shock. For someone with a religious upbringing, the 1960s were an extremely difficult time. Even though religion was a big part of the civil rights and peace movements, in my college religion was treated as irrelevant, hopelessly stodgy, and behind the times.

Feisal Abdul Rauf

I could never muster the courage to speak to girls in my college in Pune. Most of them were Parsis and spoke English. I came from a village and could barely converse in English.

Sharad Pawar

I was a teacher for a long time. I taught at a community college: voice, theory, humanities. And nowadays, music education is a dying thing. Funding is being cut more and more and more.

Jon Secada

We kinda look at this as the second or third chapter of our lives. After college, most people figure out what they want to do with their lives. But we already know what we want to do in the future and that is to continue to further our business goals.

Mary-Kate Olsen

In college, I had a crush on one of my professors. I used to bat my eyelashes and coo at him. He didn't respond at all, which made me like him even more.

Navi Rawat

I went to a Presbyterian college, you know, I was in... all the way, and so I remember doing my first sermon when I was 17, I was in high school. It wasn't a full twenty-five minute sermon, but for like ten minutes I got up and they let me do that, and it was on faith.

Woody Harrelson

While I was at college studying design I decided to paint. I was also greatly inspired by the colours that I had seen on my travels in the Brazilian Rain forest.

John Dyer

I want to go to college, and I want to keep acting and singing.

Miranda Cosgrove

I remember being in college knowing I didn't want to go anymore. I wanted to try and become an actor. There is a something in me, with a risk of sounding cliche, that I just had to do it. I knew from an early age that acting was my path.

Jake Gyllenhaal

The only reason I got into broadcasting was, I needed money to pay for my junior and senior years at college, and they hired me, those fools!

Alex Trebek

Knowledge goes hand-in-hand with truth - something I learned with a bit of tough love from my Jesuit education first at Regis High School in New York City and then at Holy Cross College in Worcester, Mass.

Anthony Fauci

College atheletes used to get a degree in bringing your pencil.

Ruby Wax

Just because someone has gone to an elite school and college does not make him smarter than the person who has grown up on street knowledge.

Vikas Swarup

The college that takes students with modest entering abilities and improves their abilities substantially contributes more than the school that takes very bright students and helps them develop only modestly.

Derek Bok

When I was in college, I became interested in various aspects of foreign policy and international relations. Even as a kid, I was interested in what I call, loosely speaking, forbidden knowledge.

Barry Eisler

Americans in particular are myopic. They're not traveling as much. When you were a college student, the next thing you would do on graduation was to take a year off and travel. That's what I did. I went to Indonesia.

Julie Taymor

I ran through most of college and ran through most of grad school. When I was writing my dissertation for my Ph.D., it was literally the only hour of the day that I wasn't working. It was nine months of torture, but I made sure I got out to run.

Jane McGonigal

No, I never went to college. Always regretted it, always envied people who did.

Sydney Pollack

Get your product in front of actual, living, breathing strangers. Your college roommate's approval does not mean there's market demand.

Kathryn Minshew

I guess as long as people think of me for different ages, I'll trust their opinion. I remember noticing one year that Michelle Monaghan played 34 and 19, so I've kind of clung to that as my justification that I can be Jake Gyllenhaal's wife and a freshman in college in the same year.

Anna Kendrick

College is part of the American dream. It shouldn't be part of a financial nightmare for families.

Barbara Mikulski

But yeah, I played bass guitar in high school and in college and then I actually fractured my thumb, so my bass career went bye-bye.

Colin Hanks

But my manners also came from when I was in college and began participating in critiques. You have to speak with someone respectfully about their work and be honest and open, without hurting them.

Tim Gunn

I had no choice but to work hard. I was a straight-A student, went to college, and I loved business. I never thought I was going to be a singer myself. It came accidentally.

Jenni Rivera

I played college soccer before I was hurt, and just to be able to jump back into something that you could be so competitive at or you can achieve, to get to the Paralympics, that's the first really big achievement that you can have. It's the second biggest sporting event in the world. To be a part of it and to get a medal for that, it's unreal.

Mark Zupan

I was very fascinated with meteorology at a young age. I lived on the Gulf Coast and hurricanes blew through there. That is the class I failed in college: meteorology.

Jim Parsons

I graduated from Bowdoin College and went to the Harvard Graduate School of Education. Then I left and took a job teaching really poor inner-city white kids in Boston. It was interesting to me because I'd never been around poor whites before.

Geoffrey Canada

We want people to realize you are at a design school, not a land grant college. The way we look says a great deal about who we are.

James Hall

In college, I was a weather anchor for the local news. I would 'borrow' my forecast from The Weather Channel.

Emily Procter

When students leave college, they are like children who know nothing about the problems of life, and don't have a political stance.

Oscar Niemeyer

I entered the literary world, really, from outside. My entire background has been in sciences; I was a biology major in college, then went to medical school. I've never had any formal training in writing.

Khaled Hosseini

Most people have an aversion to risk, my college economics professor told me. Which means they have to be rewarded to take on that risk. The higher the risk, the higher the possible payout has to be for people to jump.

Michael Arrington

As my father would have said, I went through the college of hard knocks.

Gloria Allred

Imagine filling a college with the first 1,000 students to get perfect SATs. Whatever the racial composition of that class would be, the notion seems absurd because we know that college in America is supposed to be about creating citizens and leaders in a diverse nation.

Eric Liu

Dad was a chemistry professor at Saint Olaf College in Minnesota, then Oxford College in Minnesota, and a very active member of the American Chemical Society education committee, where he sat on the committee with

Linus Pauling, who had authored a very phenomenally important textbook of chemistry.

Peter Agre

While I was in college becoming a good Catholic I was also becoming a writer - one haunted by Catholicism.

Julianna Baggott

I was in college in Washington, D.C. I did three years full-time. I did all my requirements, and my senior year was really a gut year. And I said, 'Law school will always be there.' I was in no hurry to get right into that.

Alec Baldwin

I went to military college in Canada and graduated as an officer in the Navy but also as an engineer.

Marc Garneau

Coming out of college with a degree in fine arts and painting isn't worth much any more.

Dan Fogelberg

My first summer in college I worked in a fruit fly lab where I had two jobs: dissect the fruit fly larvae brains and incinerate the old tubes of flies.

Emily Oster

Unfortunately, the elimination of incentives such as parole, good time credits and funding for college courses, means that fewer inmates participate in and excel in literacy, education, treatment and other development programs.

Bobby Scott

When you start at catering college, nobody prepares you for a book tour or public speaking.

Rene Redzepi

I could describe my career in two words: who knew. I was on the path to becoming a professional baseball player, but I got injured in college. When I decided to move out to L.A. to try acting, nobody was betting on me, not even my family.

Shemar Moore

I have a weird vision of relationships because my parents have known each other since second grade, and they got married right out of college.

Dakota Fanning

One of the wonderful things about going to a small college is you can get into everything.

Art Linkletter

The thing that drives most coaches out of coaching in college is they get tired of the grind of recruiting.

Bobby Bowden

One suggestion my wife and I have used in our personal finance courses we teach at college is simply writing down all expenditures and seeing where the money goes. That alone will cause heads of households to think twice about x, y or z expenditure, and to consider carefully whether they really need something or not.

Mark Skousen

Student loan debt is the reason I don't advise students who want to become entrepreneurs to apply to elite, expensive colleges. They can be as successful if they go to a relatively inexpensive public college.

Vivek Wadhwa

Some of my finest memories are from my time at the University of Texas. College baseball, I love it.

Roger Clemens

If you offer athletes stipends, then you're into pay-for-play, and that's the ballgame. People should realize that, and they should realize that amateurism never has been a sustainable model for a sports-entertainment industry. It wasn't in tennis. It wasn't in the Olympics. And it's not in big-time college sports.

Charlie Pierce

I was 16 when I got admission in Hans Raj College. I completed school when I was 16, so everyone in my class -

Zoology Honours batch 92 - was 18, and I was often treated like a kid.

Anurag Kashyap

When I went to college, my goal was to be a college history teacher. I majored in history.

George J. Mitchell

I was always kind of a school person - my parents were teachers, and my grandparents were immigrants, so their big thing was, 'Go to college, go to college, go to college.'

Mayim Bialik

I've always enjoyed drinking wine, ever since I was in college. My appreciation really took off when I began to visit Napa. I was toying with an idea of making wine in Napa, but it's prohibitively expensive, and the competition is fierce.

Kyle MacLachlan

When our markets work, people throughout our economy benefit - Americans seeking to buy a car or buy a home, families borrowing to pay for college, innovators borrowing on the strength of a good idea for a new product or technology, and businesses financing investments that create new jobs.

Henry Paulson

I was only in college, unfortunately, for, um, a year. I think my major was public relations, and I had no idea what it meant except it seemed maybe attainable.

James L. Brooks

Going to college is neither necessary nor sufficient to be well-educated.

Alex Tabarrok

I strongly support extending current student loan interest rates and increasing the college tuition tax credit for students and their families.

Scott Howell

The greatest challenge I think is adjusting to not playing baseball. The reason for that is I had to come out of baseball and come into the business world, not being a college graduate, not being educated to come into the business world the way I should have.

Willie Mays

By playing on people's desire to belong to groups, Facebook creates a new, inclusive society. After all, Facebook is not like Harvard College. Anyone with access to the Internet can sign up.

Amity Shlaes

I had the notion that I wanted to write the great dirty American novel, so I went to Roanoke College on the GI Bill.

Tom T. Hall

My mother never asked me whether I wanted to go to college, but told me I was going - to the University of Maryland on an academic scholarship.

Gayle Tzemach Lemmon

I never really drank coffee in college, but now I'm on my feet all day and out all night and can't believe it hasn't always been in my life. When morning comes I crave it.

Gail Simmons

If I didn't have a scholarship to go to the University of Florida or any school, I probably would have considered the military because my family could not afford to send me to college.

Emmitt Smith

I made it to London aged six, an event I recorded in my diary with coloured markers to convey my sense of occasion. And in 1983, after graduating from college, I returned to spend two years at Cambridge University.

Jean Hanff Korelitz

I did everything I could to stay in college and pay my own way, so I think that if success hadn't come so quickly, I would still be pursuing it.

Moira Kelly

Cote de Pablo is one of my best friends! We went to college together.

Matt Bomer

I was born in Evanston, Illinois. I spent my elementary and part of my junior high school years in a D.C. suburb. And then I spent my high school years in Minnesota. And then I spent my college years in Colorado. And then I spent some time living in China. And then I spent three years in Vermont before moving down to Nashville.

Abigail Washburn

I grew up in the age of discount air fare, and for me, the act of joining a culture was a great way about learning about that different culture. So I grew up in the South, and went to college in the North, and found out that I learned about myself as a Southerner by leaving the South and going to the Northeast.

Bruce Feiler

The fact is that everybody around a college basketball game - the coaches, the announcers, even the referees at a lower level - calculates when the game is really over. They calculate it with intuition and guesswork.

Bill James

I have no urge to go back to college.

Kristin Cavallari

I did 'The Karate Kid,' then I just went back to college. I didn't know how much money it made and I didn't have a publicist. I didn't have any sense of the business part of it.

Elisabeth Shue

I snap with my mom. It was a great way for me to see my dog when I was in college. We send selfies, too.

Evan Spiegel

My father would not pay for me to study anything but engineering or math in college.

Teri Hatcher

Getting through high school and college was one of my greatest achievements.

Ann Bancroft

I didn't take the typical path and go to college after high school. Instead, I saved up money from teaching dance classes and moved to L.A. But my family was so supportive - I never felt pressure from them. It's crucial to find a support system, even if it's not your family.

Dianna Agron

I grew up in a very small, close-knit, Southern Baptist family, where everything was off-limits. So I couldn't wait to get to college and have some fun. And I did for the first two years. And I regret a lot of it, because my grades were in terrible shape. I never got in serious trouble, except for my grades.

John Grisham

I realized that I was African when I came to the United States. Whenever Africa came up in my college classes, everyone turned to me. It didn't matter whether the subject was Namibia or Egypt; I was expected to know, to explain.

Chimamanda Ngozi Adichie

I finished high school, moved to Nashville for college, and set out to break into the music business. Every night when I called home with news of my experiences, my mom and dad would encourage me to keep taking those small steps.

Trisha Yearwood

When I left college, I was out of work for three years. I had this dream of being on 'SNL,' and that was all I could imagine.

Josh Gad

When you think of intelligence, don't think of a college professor; think of human beings as opposed to chimpanzees. If you don't have human intelligence, you're not even in the game.

Eliezer Yudkowsky

When I graduated from college in early 2010, I decided that I needed to create a calling card, some kind of business card that people can link to my name and face. So I did this 'Mad Men Theme Song...With a Twist' music video. I released it just as I moved to L.A.

Allison Williams

I am obsessed with story. I had a late awakening in life. In college was the first time that I understood what you could do with a story and what a good novel is - literary value and subtext and irony and everything.

Shane Carruth

When I was in college in Philly, there was a lot of post-punks... hardcore... like, rock. Sixties, retro, proto-Strokes kind of bands.

Tim Heidecker

I was called to audition for a play when I was very young, following which I continued to act as well as write and direct. When I moved to Delhi and joined Hindu College, theatre became a very big part of my life.

Imtiaz Ali

The cost of college should never discourage anyone from going after a valuable degree.

Arne Duncan

When I got to Grinnell College, I was part of the black turtleneck sweater and Camel cigarette crowd of poets and writers.

Peter Coyote

The College Access and Opportunity Act addresses the important need to make higher education more affordable and easier to access for low and middle-income students.

Ron Lewis

I always knew I wanted to be in films but didn't want anyone to taunt my parents. So I excelled in studies. I was a topper in school and college, so when I decided to become a model, people said, 'Oh your daughter is modeling,' so at least my parents could say, 'Yeah but she also came first in class.'

Anushka Sharma

I was always the frugal kid growing up because I was saving for college. Or I was always that kid that was like, 'I'm going to save my babysitting money so I can eat an expensive dinner when I go to Europe.'

Shailene Woodley

I got quite the college experience.

Ryan Cabrera

My college, Fitzwilliam, was pretty good but unfashionable and I lived in digs so I was not part of the cloistered 'old college' environment, which frankly was a bit intimidating. But I worked hard and settled in by exploring politics and girls.

Vince Cable

When I was in college, my whole goal was to write for the 'Village Voice,' and I think I was doing that by the time I was twenty-one or twenty, so everything else has kind of been gravy, you know?

Neil Strauss

They should have a rule: in order to be a sportswriter, you have to have played that sport, at some level; high school, college, junior college, somewhere. Or, you should have had to have been around the game for a long time.

Oscar Robertson

We need to make college affordable in price, and also have lower-cost student loans and more available grants for students.

Debbie Stabenow

I have no ax to grind. I was lucky. I played. How many guys play high school, college football never play pro football?

Art Donovan

I've studied Chinese in college, but basically, I'm not bilingual.

David Henry Hwang

Condoleezza Rice, the national security adviser, is right there... she's in town because her father was at Johnson Smith College... and she was delivering a speech there.

Al Michaels

I throw better than anybody in college and I can throw with anybody in the pros. There, that's what I think.

Dan Marino

In college, my friend Melanie and I used to have weekly Jimmy Stewart viewings, and 'Harvey' seemed to make its way into the rotation an inordinate amount of times.

Rich Sommer

In the early '90s, I was disillusioned after the blasts and riots in Mumbai. I was in college and started thinking that religion was the root cause of all these evils. While my father told me not to blame religion because of a few bad people, I wasn't convinced. The faith was restored after I started writing my first book.

Amish Tripathi

The only trouble here is they won't let us study enough. They are so afraid we shall break down and you know the reputation of the College is at stake, for the question is, can girls get a college degree without ruining their health?

Ellen Swallow Richards

I always think I know the way a novel will go. I write maps on oversized art pads like the kind I carried around in college when I was earnest about drawing. I need to have some idea of the shape of the novel, where its headed, so that I can proceed with confidence. But the truth is my characters start doing and saying things I don't expect.

Julianna Baggott

I got out of college and I went to get my master's in creative writing at San Francisco State. I was working as an actor at the Actor's Workshop, being abused as a intern.

Peter Coyote

If I had to give one piece of advice to incoming college freshmen, I'd say always be true to yourself.

Beverley Mitchell

It's that way all the way down the line. I've got a boy coaching college ball and another son coaching high school. All the way down to summer leagues, all the way down to kids who are 14 years old. All those teams have a closer.

Bruce Sutter

In college I didn't dress up every day, for class or stuff like that, but when it came time to do certain things I'd dress up for sure.

Russell Westbrook

Playing college soccer was going to be the top of my athletic feats. I wasn't going to the Olympics. I was a decent player, but it's because of hard work, not because I was Freddy Adu. I wouldn't have a medal from the Olympics if I wasn't in a chair. I wouldn't have gone to the Olympics and experienced the whole atmosphere.

Mark Zupan

Up until college age I was using the typical little-boy dummy that sits on the knee and makes woodpecker jokes.

My first original character didn't happen until later, and that was Jose the Jalapeno on a Stick.

Jeff Dunham

Back in college, I remember shooting stupid videos with my friends. It would be us going around town in capes pretending we were superheroes.

Anders Holm

I knew in my gut that there was something wrong with a system that couldn't fire its incompetents, and I had my share of incompetent college teachers.

Luke Ford

I graduated from a place called Whitworth College in Spokane with a theater degree, then in 1993 I moved to L.A. and auditioned and did very well there. My first gig was playing a skinhead in John Singleton's 'Higher Learning', and I played Glenn Close's son in a TV movie called 'Serving In Silence.'

Trevor St. John

I was in college, and very disappointed. I majored in commercial art and interior design for three or four years. At that time, it seemed the thing I really wanted to do, production design, just wasn't available in the U.K., so I turned to music.

Eric Burdon

My mom played tennis for, like, six hours a day and went to college on a tennis scholarship, because that was the way she could go to school. So they instilled in me the idea that you have to work hard for the things you want in life and never complain.

Dakota Fanning

Originally, I think, I wanted to be an actor. But I got into broadcasting by accident, if you will, because I needed money to pay for my college education. I applied for a summer announcing job at a couple of radio stations.

Alex Trebek

When I finish as the host of 'Jeopardy!' I'm going to go up to Taft in central California. They have a small college there that teaches you about oil drilling.

Alex Trebek

High school and college were my punk, formative years. I was playing hardcore, learning to be a musician. In bands, you tour, but you're paid nothing; you're playing to 50 people in a basement, sleeping in a van, and you love it.

Steve Aoki

I didn't want to be a dancer. I just did it to work my way through college. But I was always an athlete and gymnast, so it came naturally.

Gene Kelly

And when I started college, I think I was good at two things: arguing and asking questions.

Karen Hughes

I studied French in high school and German in college and I once took a 24-hour Italian crash course. English has by far the most words in it of any other language. Our money might not be worth anything anymore, but the language is.

Roy Blount, Jr.

I don't recall any interest in science in particular. It came later in college.

Ellen Ochoa

My parents are from Ghana. Until I was 17, I thought you had to go to college. I had no idea. I didn't know it was not an option.

Ato Essandoh

You go to college not only for the latest knowledge but also to meet people from different backgrounds. That's the genius of the American higher-education system compared with the Europeans'. We don't simply skim the elite.

Donna Shalala

I never took my SAT's. I never applied to college. I moved right out here and jumped into the thick of things. Whether that was the smart move or not, I'm sitting here talking to you now, so it paid off.

Scott Foley

My ambition was to be cosmopolitan. I grew up in the suburbs. I went to college in Maine. I had a dream in my head that if you wanted to be the most urbane, living-life-to-the-fullest kind of person, Paris was the place to be.

Rosecrans Baldwin

My very first acting job ever, the first time I got paid to be an actress, was in 2001, right between my sophomore and junior year in college, when I was just 19 years old. I got paid $250 every two weeks, 10 shows a week, to be in the Utah Shakespearean Festival. I was Calpurnia in 'Julius Caesar.'

Katy Mixon

I was an English major in college, took a ton of creative writing courses, and was a newspaper reporter for 10 years.

Jennifer Weiner

The student community of Presidency College was also politically most active.

Amartya Sen

I studied the Bible and philosophy in college, and I think in a certain sense that's the kind of stuff that still makes my brain work.

Win Butler

If you want to be a doctor, a lawyer you must go to college. But if you want to be a musician or such, study your craft. Study music.

Billy Eckstine

My favorite NBA team are the houston rockets and favorite college team are the duke blue devils.

Dante Hall

There is no formula to making it to the NFL other than good fortune and and playing well in college.

Dante Hall

Growing up in college, in high school, I was the focal point.

James Harden

I played bass guitar in high school and in college and then I actually fractured my thumb, so my bass career went bye-bye.

Colin Hanks

I wanted to go to medical school. But, I never got a college scholarship.

Edwin Moses

I went to Moorehouse College. There was no track and field there.

Edwin Moses

I worry about putting food on the table, paying for my kids needs, their college fees in years to come. It's about earning enough to have a living to be able to look after your children.

Shane Filan

I decided that I didn't want to spend my time in a liberal arts college.

Chick Corea

My first year of college was tough. I thought that just being an athlete I could get by. I thought I was okay until I got kicked out, which happened twice.

Victor Cruz

I got a degree in sociology, didn't read much fiction in college, and I was a pretty political, left-wing type of guy. I wanted to do some kind of work in social change and make things better for the poor man, and I was very romantic and passionate about it.

Andre Dubus III

I kept thinking, I went to college and I have to get a real job.

Mary Chapin Carpenter

Pre-teens, teens and college students have unlimited access to the Internet - 24 hours a day, seven days a week. Because of the repeated exposure they have to illegal Internet gambling sites, they fall victim by the thousands.

Spencer Bachus

After college, I went to San Francisco and worked as a secretary in a reinsurance company. That was a pretty dismal job. It was a real small place. Guys would come in, and they'd sort of stick out their arms like wings so I could take their coats off. They'd tell me, 'Two,' and I'd put two lumps of sugar in their coffee.

William T. Vollmann

The minimum wage is not something that you want to stay on as a permanent basis. For example, if you have a minimum wage job, you don't stay there 20 or 30 years. You don't put your children through college working on minimum wage.

John Raese

I'm sure there were times when I wish I had thought, 'Gosh, that might really embarrass mom and dad,' but our parents didn't raise us to think about them. They're very selfless and they wanted us to have as normal of a college life as possible. So really, we didn't think of any repercussions.

Jenna Bush

My parents being Bengali, we always had music in our house. My nani was a trained classical singer, who taught my mum, who, in turn, was my first teacher. Later I would travel almost 70 kms to the nearest town, Kota, to learn music from my guru Mahesh Sharmaji, who was also the principal of the music college there.

Shreya Ghoshal

I did an internship at the Ardent theatre company in Philly after dropping out of college. I was earning $165 a week building sets and cleaning the toilets. Cleaning toilets is a good way of getting in touch with your creativity. That's when you find out if you got anything going on in your head.

Jill Scott

In the 2000 presidential election, Al Gore got more votes than George W. Bush, but still lost the election. The Supreme Court's ruling in Florida gave Bush that pivotal state, and doomed Gore to lose the Electoral College. That odd scenario - where the candidate with the most votes loses - has happened three times in U.S. history.

Juan Williams

I went to college on a classical piano scholarship. My grandmother made me practice one full hour a day. Every day. Man. I thought all she wanted was for me not to have any fun. Next thing you know, you have a career in music. Now, not everybody's going to go on and be Mozart or Michael Jackson. But music makes you smarter.

Jamie Foxx

I was a pitcher, shortstop and outfielder, and the Yankees tried to sign me out of high school as a first-round draft pick in 1981. I turned them down to go to college.

Bo Jackson

After I graduated from school, I enrolled in the military college, a cadet school. This is the first stage of military training; it instills discipline and various qualities required for military life.

Roman Romanenko

I'm proud to be part of the Dr. Pepper Scholarship Giveaway. It's a great program that gives me the chance to brighten the day for some lucky college students with free tuition.

Lou Holtz

I was going to go to a four-year college and be an anthropologist or to an art school and be an illustrator when a friend convinced me to learn photography at the University of Southern California. Little did I know it was a school that taught you how to make movies! It had never occurred to me that I'd ever have any interest in filmmaking.

George Lucas

During Vietnam, I was in college, enjoying my student deferment. The government wisely felt that, in my case, military service was less important than completing my studies to prepare me for my chosen career: comedian.

Al Franken

If you have four years to complete your college education, do it.

Bo Jackson

When I went to college, as much as my parents emphasized academic achievement, they emphasized marriage even more. They told me that the most eligible women marry young to get a 'good man' before they are all taken.

Sheryl Sandberg

My dad was a composer and a musician, but he never finished high school. His formal education was rather minimal from the standards of today's college graduates and Ph.D.'s, but he had a deep interest in questions of science and questions of the universe.

Brian Greene

I spent my first two years at a small all-male college in Virginia called Hampden-Sydney. That was like going to college 120 years ago. The languages, a year of rhetoric, all of the great books, Western Man courses, stuff like that.

Stephen Colbert

Some of George W. Bush's friends say that Bush believes God called him to be president during these times of trial. But God told me that He/She/It had actually chosen Al Gore by making sure that Gore won the popular vote and, God thought, the Electoral College. 'That worked for everyone else,' God said.

Al Franken

Almost every college playwright or sketch or improv comedian was sort of aware of Christopher Durang - even kids in high school. His short plays were so accessible to younger people and I think that was inspirational to me.

Mindy Kaling

We should all feel confident in our intelligence. By the way, intelligence to me isn't just being book-smart or having a college degree; it's trusting your gut instincts, being intuitive, thinking outside the box, and sometimes just realizing that things need to change and being smart enough to change it.

Tabatha Coffey

I began to understand the challenges that first-generation college students and students of color have in college.

Freeman A. Hrabowski III

I've teamed up with one of the headmasters at Eton College, and we're spearheading a kind of "slow education movement in Britain. It's based on this idea of moving away from the fast-food approach to learning and going to something deeper, more woolly, harder to measure.

Carl Honore

Most of the time I liked school and got good grades. In junior high, though, I hit a stumbling block with math - I used to come home and cry because of how frustrated I was! But after a few good teachers and a lot of perseverance, I ended up loving math and even choosing it as a major when I got to college.

Danica McKellar

I've been thinking of humorous things since I was... I can't remember when. All the way through elementary school, all the way through junior high, all the way through high school, through college and after college, I was thinking of the same kinds of things that I say in front of an audience now.

Steven Wright

All of my friends who have younger siblings who are going to college or high school - my number one piece of advice is: You should learn how to program.

Mark Zuckerberg

Since most American students cannot simply pay their full tuition out of pocket, financing a college education often takes the form of loans, both private and from the government.

Charles B. Rangel

I was in school, but I wasn't into school. I wasn't doing what I wanted to be doing in school, which was film studies. That was what I intended on doing, but I didn't go away to a university because I wanted to stay in L.A. and audition while I took classes, so I elected to go to a community college and just take G.E. courses. It was terrible.

Dylan O'Brien

I didn't want to go down any scarier path of low self-esteem than I was already on the track for. So during my second year of college I was like, 'I'm over it! I have to go see what this other thing called life is about!'

Anna Chlumsky

It's funny, but when I arrived in California to start college I was much more interested in becoming a surfer and cruise along in life from one beach to the next. I didn't plan out any huge career for myself.

Benicio Del Toro

At 17, I signed a recording contract right out of high school, so I started touring and traveling the world. I sort of missed out on the college experience.

Tommy Lee

When I grew up I always wanted to act. Also, I wanted to be either a lawyer or a doctor. However, when I got to college and realized what those occupations entailed, I changed my mind real quick.

Tia Mowry

I went to Jersey City State College to please a family member. I wasn't prepared for school. To say I failed out is putting it nicely.

Derek Luke

When I went to college, I majored in American literature, which was unusual then. But it meant that I was broadly exposed to nineteenth-century American literature. I became interested in the way that American writers used metaphoric language, starting with Emerson.

Marilynne Robinson

The essays in The Great Taos Bank Robbery were my project to win a Master of Arts degree in English when I quit being a newspaper editor and went back to college.

Tony Hillerman

Going from college to being on national TV almost fresh outta school, it happened really fast.

Terrence J

My sister started acting professionally when she was twelve, but I wanted to go to college first.

Rooney Mara

Although becoming a singer was my plan A after first hearing Whitney Houston when I was 17, I started off with plan B by going to the teacher-training college that my dad went to. It was a slow coming of age.

Toni Braxton

I never really took a proper art class in college. I just started reading art magazines and going to galleries. I was really drawn to it.

Larry Gagosian

Credit card companies pay college students generously to stand outside dining halls, dorms, and academic buildings and encourage their fellow students to apply for credit cards.

Louise Slaughter

It is strange when you're a loser in college, which I was, to then get your own show.

Topher Grace

I could be happy doing something like architecture. It would involve another couple of years of graduate school, but that's what I studied in college. That's what I always wanted to do.

Parker Stevenson

I wanted to be an English teacher. I wanted to do it for the corduroy jackets with patches on the side. When I got to college, as I was walking across campus one day, I ripped off a little flyer for this sketch-comedy group. It ended up being one of the greatest things I've ever done.

John Krasinski

In college, I got interested in news because the world was coming apart. The civil rights movement, the antiwar movement, the women's right movement. That focused my radio ambitions toward news.

Bob Edwards

A lot of actors said they hated the studio system, but I loved it. It was like a college; it was a great place to learn.

Richard Widmark

I was an actor as a kid in Boston. Then I went to art school with Brice Marden, the Massachusetts College of Art. So the hybrid of being an actor and artist is a director.

Arne Glimcher

My background is in theater. I was a theater major in college.

Amy Schumer

Football is my profession now. I'm getting married in August... It's a new experience for me as someone just getting out of college. I still have the same attitude about football I always had. I play hard. I enjoy practice. I'd rather be throwing in passing drills than sitting around and watching TV.

Doug Flutie

I would say I was jock. I went to Sierra College. I was a big baseball player. Getting into the MLB was my dream - to become a left-handed pitcher for the Yankees. That's what I was hoping, but life kind of went the other way.

Ryan Guzman

My dad is quite possibly the biggest Giants fan in the world. I believe he wore a Phil Simms jersey to my high school and college graduations.

Bobby Moynihan

Many of our young people spend four years getting very expensive college degrees. But our universities fail them and the nation if they continue to graduate students with expertise in biochemistry, mathematics or history without teaching them to think about what problems are important and why.

Heather Wilson

I don't know if I'd call myself a prodigy, but I was a big forensics competitor in high school, and then during college I spent some time working at speech and debate camps as a coach.

Josh Gad

Cheerleading gave me a love of sports, which I brought to the Senate. I can talk to the good ol' boys about college sports because I follow it like they do.

Kay Bailey Hutchison

Being considerate of others will take your children further in life than any college degree.

Marian Wright Edelman

Believe it or not, lots of people change their majors and abandon their dreams just to avoid a couple of math classes in college.

Danica McKellar

My musical influence is really from my father. He was a DJ in college. My parents met at New York University. So he listened to, you know, Motown, and he listened to Bob Dylan. He listened to Grateful Dead and Rolling Stones, but he also listened to reggae music. And he collected vinyl.

Talib Kweli

A church without women would be like the apostolic college without Mary. The Madonna is more important than the apostles, and the church herself is feminine, the spouse of Christ and a mother.

Pope Francis

Rich people never go to war. You ask a college kid to go to war, and he's like, 'Umm, I'm taking this sociology class, and I think war is, like, really stupid, and my roommate's, like, half Afghani, so it's going to cause some static.'

Bill Burr

I'm thinking of a legacy that I can be proud of and wealth that my grandchildren can use to go to college. So world domination - in terms of providing for my family - is absolutely my goal.

Nicki Minaj

Kids go to school and college and get through, but they don't seem to really care about using their minds. School doesn't have the kind of long term positive impact that it should.

Howard Gardner

My mama told me in college, 'I love you, and you're God's child, but natural beauty will only take you so far.'

Robin Roberts

No one likes the Electoral College, expect perhaps those who were elected because of it. No one likes gerrymandering, except those doing the gerrymandering.

No one likes the filibuster, except those doing the filibustering.

Kevin Bleyer

Never get married in college; it's hard to get a start if a prospective employer finds you've already made one mistake.

Elbert Hubbard

Every time a student walks past a really urgent, expressive piece of architecture that belongs to his college, it can help reassure him that he does have that mind, does have that soul.

Louis Kahn

I think if I were a college professor, no one would say I was uncomfortable about being shy because that might be expected. But I think because of people's stereotypes, they think of a football player as someone who is very outgoing and I'm not.

Ricky Williams

I studied Japanese language and culture in college and graduate school, and afterward went to work in Tokyo, where I met a young man whose father was a famous businessman and whose mother was a geisha. He and I never discussed his parentage, which was an open secret, but it fascinated me.

Arthur Golden

I was born in Harlem, raised in the South Bronx, went to public school, got out of public college, went into the Army, and then I just stuck with it.

Colin Powell

The best math lesson we can teach college students this year is to subtract a tuition increase and benefit from the dividends of higher education.

Jodi Rell

Every step, whether at high school or at college or at the NFL, I had to climb and crawl and scratch to get there.

Victor Cruz

I think if you're a good high school player that you have the ability to be a good college football player. If you're a good college football then you have the ability to be a great NFL player.

Robert Griffin III

Computer games tend to be boys' games, warlike games with more violence. We have not spent enough time thinking through how to encourage more girls to be involved in computing before coming to college so they can see a possible career in information technology.

Freeman A. Hrabowski III

As a freshman in college, I was having a lot of trouble adjusting. I took a meditation class to handle anxiety. It really helped. Then as a grad student at Harvard, I was awarded a pre-doctoral traveling fellowship to India, where my focus was on the ancient systems of psychology and meditation practices of Asia.

Daniel Goleman

My son is trying to be a sports writer, and my daughter is a college student. She wants to be a comedy writer, and she's at film school. I discouraged both of them early on from getting involved in Starbucks. I didn't think it would be fair; plus, they didn't have any interest anyway.

Howard Schultz

As a high school dropout, I understand the value of education: A second chance at obtaining my high school diploma through the G.I. Bill led me to attend college and law school and allowed me the opportunity to serve in Congress.

Charles B. Rangel

I kind of got more interested in writing after I turned in my last college essay and nobody was going to tell me what kind of academic papers to write anymore. I could write whatever I wanted, and I realized that I actually liked it when I could choose what I would write.

Dan Millman

Let me say no danger and no hardship ever makes me wish to get back to that college life again.

Joshua Chamberlain

Instead of saving for someone else's college education, I'm currently saving for a luxury retirement community replete with golf carts and handsome young male nurses who love butterscotch.

Jen Kirkman

However my parents - both of whom came from impoverished backgrounds and neither of whom had been to college, took the view that my overactive imagination was an amusing quirk that would never pay a mortgage or secure a pension.

J. K. Rowling

I'm going to college. I don't care if it ruins my career. I'd rather be smart than a movie star.

Natalie Portman

I turned down a scholarship to Yale. The problem with college is that there's a tendency to mistake preparation for productivity. You can prepare all you want, but if you never roll the dice you'll never be successful.

Shia LaBeouf

I wanted to race cars. I didn't like school, and all I wanted to do was work on cars. But right before I graduated, I got into a really bad car accident, and I spent that summer in the hospital thinking about where I was heading. I decided to take education more seriously and go to a community college.

George Lucas

When I was in college, my school newspaper accepted an ad from a Holocaust revisionist organization. This would have been offensive on most college campuses across the country, but I went to a school with a very large Jewish population, so the ad, as you might expect, stirred absolute outrage.

Simon Sinek

I went to college. I had a double major in biology and physical education, but my major was wrestling.

Dan Gable

I had a lot of success from the start. I never really was tested for long periods of time. I got my first professional job while I was a senior in college. I signed with the William Morris Agency before I graduated.

Denzel Washington

You're not a bad parent if you don't save for your kid's college because instead you had to choose to feed them and clothe them. Those things come first. They can go to school and do this thing called 'work' while they're in school.

Dave Ramsey

I didn't dream about being a director. I didn't know I wanted to do something with film until the summer between my sophomore and junior years at Morris College in Atlanta, Georgia.

Spike Lee

You always give credit where credit is due - to high school coaches, college coaches - but my dad, the foundation that he built with me, is where all of this came from. The speed, the determination, the mindset, just the natural belief that

you can do anything you put your mind to, it all comes
from my dad.

Robert Griffin III

For some students, especially in the sciences, the
knowledge gained in college may be directly relevant to
graduate study. For almost all students, a liberal arts
education works in subtle ways to create a web of
knowledge that will illumine problems and enlighten
judgment on innumerable occasions in later life.

Derek Bok

I would say my fraternity was nothing but a bunch of farm
boys; we weren't really in the whole fraternity scene, but
yeah, that's a safe assessment of who I am. I've lived that
life, growing up in agriculture and then going off to college
and joining a fraternity, livin' that life.

Luke Bryan

The word survivor suggests someone who has emerged
alive from a plane crash or a natural disaster. But the word
can also refer to the loved ones of murder victims, and this

was the sense in which it was used at a four-day conference in early June at Boston College.

Godfried Danneels

In Malaysia, where Western culture was extremely influential, I'd grown up listening to Elvis and the Beatles and watching American movies. People wanted to be like Americans. In contrast, when I got here, I saw prosperous middle-class American college students wanting to somehow join the Third World.

Feisal Abdul Rauf

Until my senior year, baseball and basketball were my best sports; and even when I was a senior, I still wanted to play baseball professionally. But the family wanted me to go to college, and I guess I agreed with them, or else I would have accepted some of the offers I got.

Joe Namath

One day, my youngest uncle - the other one who was first to go to college, Randy - and I were sitting out on the front porch. And he was brilliant. He ended up - he just retired from Boeing Aircraft in Wichita, Kansas.

James Earl Jones

I never really paid attention to sports, which, coming from the mecca of football in Texas, is kind of odd. I played sports, but I was nerdy. Having a single mother, the pressure was on me to get good grades and a scholarship and go to college.

Sarah Shahi

It was depressing, very depressing. I worried about how I would make a living. I didn't want to stay on the farm. It didn't offer the challenge I wanted and yet, without a college education, I felt that I was really out of luck.

Clyde Tombaugh

My friend, Sue Ann, in college pulled me aside and said, 'Honey I love you but you have got to start waxing your eyebrows. They look wild!' So thank you , that kinda changed my life.

Angela Kinsey

The presidents of colleges have to have some courage to step forward. You can't limit alcohol in college sports, you have to get rid of it.

Dean Smith

I went to Gettysburg College, where the famous Civil War battle was fought. I majored in English. I would've liked to major in writing, but they didn't offer a major in that.

Jerry Spinelli

I picked up reading late because I grew up dyslexic. When I went to college, a friend who was a big reader got me started on a number of writers, including Hemingway.

Lee Pace

College isn't the place to go for ideas.

Helen Keller

Going to college offered me the chance to play football for four more years.

Ronald Reagan

I think all college students, maybe before college even, but certainly by college, should read 'Letters to a Young Poet.' It cuts through to the heart of what's of value in life. To really be true to your own spirit. To be awake and develop patience so that you truly understand what it is you're trying to do, desire, and who in fact you really are.

Alice Walker

When bright young minds can't afford college, America pays the price.

Arthur Ashe

I quit college so fast I didn't even clean out my locker.

Steven Spielberg

You can't have a university without having free speech, even though at times it makes us terribly uncomfortable. If students are not going to hear controversial ideas on college campuses, they're not going to hear them in America. I believe it's part of their education.

Donna Shalala

College graduates should not have to live out their 20s in their childhood bedrooms, staring up at fading Obama posters and wondering when they can move out and get going with life.

Paul Ryan

To compete in a global economy, our students must continue their education beyond high school. To make this expectation a reality, we must give students the tools they need to succeed, including the opportunity to take a college entrance exam.

Jennifer Granholm

Just because I don't have a college degree doesn't mean I am not smart!

Emma Stone

After immersing myself in the mysteries of the Electoral College for a novel I wrote in the '90s, I came away believing that the case for scrapping it is less obvious than I originally thought.

Jeff Greenfield

It's great to talk about how good things are now. But we can't sit on our laurels and expect that our time will sustain itself if we don't do a better job on issues like education... It's absolutely the case that the low cost of college tuition that I was able to enjoy and the financial aid I was able to receive made my education possible.

Wendy Davis

I'm in college at North Carolina State University. I'm about to start my sophomore year and have an apartment on campus with three buddies I've grown up with. I get to be normal when I'm there, and then I tour Thursday through Sunday.

Scotty McCreery

The institutions of college athletics exist primarily as unreality fueled by deceit. The unreality is that universities should be in the business of providing large spectacles of mass entertainment. The fundamental absurdity of that notion requires the promulgation of the various deceits necessary to carry it out.

Charlie Pierce

Everything I learned about the Great Depression was from a college textbook.

Ralph Abernathy

I had acne late, in college. My skin used to be really flawless. Went to college, became a vegetarian, ate a lot of cheese - big mistake. Here I am trying to be healthy and I'm eating grilled cheese sandwiches and french fries every day, having mad eruptions all over my face.

Wesley Snipes

My father died during open-heart surgery on March 29 of my senior year in college. I was getting set to go to law school. I remember sitting in the waiting room when the doctor walked in. I said to myself, The worst possible thing just happened. What will you do?

Steve Wynn

Reed College required a thesis for a Bachelor's degree. Normally a Bachelor's is sort of like being stamped 'Prime US Beef.' They just walk you through, hand out the diplomas and you fill in your name later on.

David Eddings

Unemployment rates among Americans who never went to college are about double that of those who have a postsecondary education.

Bill Gates

What destroys more self-confidence than any other educational thing in America is being assigned to some remedial math when you get into some college, and then it's not taught very well and you end up with this sense of, 'Hey, I can't really figure those things out.'

Bill Gates

Seriousness is stupidity sent to college.

P. J. O'Rourke

I couldn't go to college, so I went to the library three days a week for 10 years.

Ray Bradbury

When I was a college student and I got interested in linguistics the concern among students was, this is a lot of fun, but after we have done a structural analysis of every language in the world what's left? It was assumed there were basically no puzzles.

Noam Chomsky

I believe that we parents must encourage our children to become educated, so they can get into a good college that we cannot afford.

Dave Barry

We never had it as rough as the kids have it today. Look at the price of a gallon of gas or a piece of real estate or a college education.

Suze Orman

I've always thought of myself as a cattle-handling specialist, a college professor first; autism is secondary.

Temple Grandin

I accidentally forgot to graduate from college.

Anne Lamott

By going to the movies, and because of other things, too, going to college, making a wide variety of friends, moving around traveling, I became a lot more open-minded than the heritage I was born into might have suggested.

Roger Ebert

Millions of young Americans have graduated from college during the Obama presidency, ready to use their gifts and get moving in life. Half of them can't find the work they studied for, or any work at all. So here's the question: Without a change in leadership, why would the next four years be any different from the last four years?

Paul Ryan

I was always the youngest person in class, skinny, scrawny, no good at sports. I asserted myself by being smart. But then I got to college and started to get C's and D's. That was fantastic. I no longer had to be the smartest person in the room.

Douglas Coupland

Yes, your kids should go to school. No, you shouldn't bankroll their degree whatever the cost. You've spent your life creating a sound financial plan; don't upend it by suspending your retirement savings or taking out a home equity line of credit to pay for a pricey college.

Suze Orman

Hospitals are closing across the country due to the burden of illegal immigration, college students find that summer jobs have dried up due to illegal immigration, and wages across the board are depressed by the overwhelming influx of cheap and illegal labor.

Elton Gallegly

Ferdinand was a gold trader. He was a lawyer for mining companies. When he entered politics in 1949, he had tons and tons of gold. When Bill Gates was a college dropout, Ferdinand already possessed billions of dollars and tons of gold. It wasn't stolen.

Imelda Marcos

The media love to cover black people on the front page. After all, when you live in a society that will lock up about 30 percent of all black men at some time in their lives and send more of them to prison than to college, chances are a fair number of those black faces will end up in the newspaper.

Michael Moore

College is the reward for surviving high school. Most people have great fun stories from college and nightmare stories from high school.

Judd Apatow

If I'd stayed at college I would have become a teacher.

Syd Barrett

My father was and is a great journalist. Thirty years ago, I was studying broadcasting in college, and the problem was I wasn't nearly as good as my father. I wasn't as quick or as smart as my old man, and I realized it would be a long time before I was ever going to be, and I decided to do something else.

George Clooney

Christ, seven years of college, down the drain.

John Belushi

When I graduated college I had a series of just humiliating jobs that I couldn't believe I was at.

Lena Dunham

So if a college education is indispensable, the challenge as I see it is how to make it more accessible.

Gordon Gee

The most obvious purpose of college education is to help students acquire information and knowledge by acquainting them with facts, theories, generalizations, principles, and the like. This purpose scarcely requires justification.

Derek Bok

My senior year of high school, when I was getting recruited for college, my dad goes to me, 'You can become an Olympic champion.' And that's the first time that I'd heard someone else say that to me. I was like, 'Uh, are you talking to me?'

Ryan Lochte

While there are many obstacles that deter students from going to college, finances by no means should be the deciding factor.

Bobby Scott

In the world today, a young lady who does not have a college education just is not educated.

Walter Annenberg

I was completely unqualified to get into Harvard. But then I went to my interview for Harvard, and the woman asked, 'Why do you want to go here?' And I took out all of my comedy writing samples that I had done. I couldn't have been more delusional in terms of what I thought they wanted in a candidate for college.

Mike Birbiglia

The internet was supposed to make this whole business of job searching rational and simple. You could post your resume and companies would search them and they'd find you. It doesn't seem to work that way. There aren't enough jobs for experienced, college educated managers and professionals.

Barbara Ehrenreich

When you ask your white friends what their cultural heritage is, they don't just say white. They give you a math equation. 'Well, I'm a third German and a fourth Irish and one-sixteenth Welsh and one-fortieth Native American for college applications.'

Hari Kondabolu

I was going to be an architect. I graduated with a degree in architecture and I had a scholarship to go back to Princeton and get my Masters in architecture. I'd done theatricals in college, but I'd done them because it was fun.

James Stewart

Really, the potential for, first of all, any college graduate today is enormously good. These are good times for anyone with a college degree today, particularly African Americans. With a college degree today, you really breach the unemployment rate.

Alexis Herman

The whole student loan thing drives me completely nuts. If it wasn't possible for 18-year-olds to sign themselves up for tens of thousands of dollars in debt in order to pay their college bills, the state governments wouldn't have found it so politically easy to cut taxpayer support for public colleges and universities.

Gail Collins

I remember when I was in college, I used to watch Julia Child's cooking show during dinner and joke with my roommates about becoming a TV chef.

Martin Yan

I attended the University of Louisville my freshman year, transferred to what was then Western Kentucky State Teachers College for my sophomore and junior years, and then graduated from the University of Louisville in the summer of 1961.

Sue Grafton

In college, before video games, we would amuse ourselves by posing programming exercises.

Ken Thompson

I remember, when I went away to college at Southern Methodist University in Dallas, my aunt sent me a book with the rules of being a Southern Belle. One of the rules was to never wear white after Labor Day. Fashion has a lot to do with confidence and making up your own rules.

Kourtney Kardashian

In many college classes, laptops depict split screens - notes from a class, and then a range of parallel stimulants: NBA playoff statistics on ESPN.com, a flight home on Expedia, a new flirtation on Facebook.

Samantha Power

I was an exchange student for a summer, and most of that summer was in Ukraine. I used to say 'the Ukraine' until I was there, and one of the Ukrainian college students I got to be good friends with, he said, 'Do you say I'm going back to the Texas,' and I said, 'No.' He said, 'We don't say we're going back to the Ukraine, either.'

Louie Gohmert

I got expelled from high school, and then did my exams from home. I decided, through that experience, that I was going to expediate my plan and didn't go to university. Instead, I went to a community college and studied the theory and history of film with the idea that I wanted to write and direct.

Charlie Hunnam

I love writing about the summer between high school and college. It's the last gasp of really being a teen.

Sarah Dessen

Football is violence and cold weather and sex and college rye.

Roger Kahn

I am here to give the American people some straight talk about higher education. Some have said we might have cut financial aid for college students. The truth is we have expanded access to college for our neediest students through the record growth of the Pell grant program.

Ric Keller

The openness of rural Nebraska certainly influenced me. That openness, in a way, fosters the imagination. But growing up, Lincoln wasn't a small town. It was a college town. It had record stores and was a liberal place.

Matthew Sweet

I have grown up in Delhi in a way, and I keep coming here often. But, and I am sorry to say, I'll always be nervous when in Delhi. In my college days, I have had my bum pinched around so many times. So yes, in Mumbai, I can just walk around and do what I want to do, but in Delhi I'll always be scared.

Preity Zinta

So while I was in college I did a little study on the freight industry, the air freight industry. And I looked at this company called Flying Tiger. And I actually put a thousand dollars in it and I remember I thought this air cargo was going to be a thing of the future.

Peter Lynch

I'm going to Columbia University but I'm trying to keep that low-profile because I don't want weird people following me there. I want the experience of normal college life.

Julia Stiles

More people are watching college football on Snapchat than they are on television.

Evan Spiegel

I came from a Hindi medium school... the principal felt that I would not fit into an English medium college. Though I was top in my class in school, and I got admission in other colleges, but I really wanted to study in St. Xavier's.

Lakshmi Mittal

I have a lot of brothers and sisters, and each movie has helped pay for tuition. And then I was like, I only have one left in college, so why am I doing this? But now I want to go back to Italy and live on a farm in Tuscany.

Rose McGowan

The way I dress, I dress totally different than I did when I was in college. I have to - try to - look professional. You change a lot when you are in the NBA, but I know where I came from.

Derrick Rose

I played piano back in my elementary school days and I sang a cappella back in college.

Masi Oka

I knew I was the second-best tennis player in the state of Florida and No. 8 in the United States of America when I was 12 years old and I couldn't tell you what I was in baseball, but I liked my chances in tennis of getting a scholarship to college.

Jim Courier

I don't remember any sibling rivalry growing up, because by the time I was really conscious, Tom was going away to college. My relationship with him, which is a very close one, really developed in more recent years.

David Hyde Pierce

In high school, I had a couple girlfriends who had very extreme eating disorders. Anorexia and bulimia. And in college as well. It's just heartbreaking. As someone going through it, it's heartbreaking. And as a friend who's helping a friend going through it, it's heartbreaking. It's a real, real disease.

Katie Lowes

When I was at college, the idea of fashion was more immediate to me, whereas art photography, the depth of it, was a different thing. Storytelling - fanciful storytelling - can only be told through fashion photography. It's the perfect way to play with fantasy and dreams.

Tim Walker

Time management is probably the biggest thing I've had to learn to deal with being on the PGA Tour, whether it be media or figuring out how many weeks to play in a row. That's been the biggest adjustment, coming from amateur and college golf.

Rickie Fowler

I was a hotshot as a junior. When I was 18, I really got into fiddling around. I completely lost interest in golf, and I guess all I could think about was going to college, getting married and having babies.

Hollis Stacy

Going through college a Red Sox fan and knowing the history behind everything that was going on back in the '80s and finally getting a chance to win a World Series for this great city and bringing it back after 86 years, it was truly special, and it's one of the highlights that I'll remember for a long time.

Tim Wakefield

When I auditioned for drama college, they asked me to do my Shakespeare. I couldn't do it. They asked me to do my modern, and I couldn't do it. They asked me if I had a song prepared, and I said 'No,' so I sang 'Happy Birthday.' And I did a reasonable improvisation, a reasonable one, nothing special at all. I don't know how I got in, but I did.

Hans Matheson

On education, in order to ensure that America remains a world leader, we must create an educated, skilled workforce in the vital areas of science, math, engineering and information technology. At the same time, we must give every student access to a college degree.

John F. Tierney

For college seniors there should be a week of being allowed to cry. Just break down and cry because you are scared and don't know what's next.

Bill Cosby

When I decided that I wanted to go to college, I wanted to be a school teacher for 7th and 8th grade boys because I felt that was an important time for them. I had gone astray at that point in my life and really wanted to help keep them from making the same mistake I had made.

Bill Cosby

www.ingramcontent.com/pod-product-compliance
Lightning Source LLC
Chambersburg PA
CBHW070633290526
45790CB00001B/81